What You Need to Know About Your Spiritual Health

Andre Antao

Copyright © 2023 Andre Antao

All rights reserved.

ISBN: 979-8-9870743-2-9

DEDICATION

In memory of my mother,

Jovita 1936-2008

CONTENTS

INTRODUTION	1
EXAMINING THE HUMAN SPIRIT OF OUR TIMES	6
A SCIENTIFIC INVESTIGATION INTO SPIRITUAL HUMAN NATURE	17
EXAMINING THE SPIRITUAL AND RELIGIOUS PHENOMENA	30
WHAT IS SPIRITUAL HEALTH	47
NEUROSCIENCE OF SPIRITUAL HEALTH	60
THE CHALLENGING TASK OF SPIRITUAL HEALTHCARE	74
HOW TO NURTURE SPIRITUAL HEALTH	88
CONCLUSION	153

INTRODUCTION

The importance of maintaining spiritual health in today's world cannot be overstated. These are very challenging times for everyone. No one escapes the overwhelming existential anxiety of our era. Everyone feels threatened by an uncertain future. The human mind is scarred by a persistent sense of suffering that remains unrelieved. Daily values, attitudes, and behaviors of people weaken the noble human spirit.

We live in a world plagued by rampant corruption and evil, including terrible atrocities, heinous crimes, gruesome violence, savage behaviors, and much more wrongdoing. The geopolitical tensions, social and economic crises, and environmental disasters make us less hopeful about a better future for humanity and the planet. It is not science fiction or fantasy; we are living in a dangerous world. Humanity seems to be on the verge of catastrophic collapse.

In the postmodern world, we see the material side of human nature dominating human life. The global culture draws people's attention away from the spiritual side of life. Materialism, consumerism, and hedonism are effectively weakening the spiritual aspect of human nature. In the pursuit of life, we show a way of living that demonstrates a lack of interest in matters related to spiritual human nature and spiritual growth.

Human culture today appears to be the biggest obstacle to developing spiritual health. In our current culture, we often fail to meaningfully engage with life and confront the ultimate questions about our human existence. We tend to ignore what truly matters in being human—shallow and fleeting goals related to the meaning and purpose of life blind us. We define the "good life" in terms of material success and hedonistic lifestyles. The "spiritual brain" appears to have a lesser influence on our human nature.

Today, we lack the "freedoms" we all desire in life. It feels impossible to tame our restless minds and spirits. Everything we do distracts us from what is happening to the human spirit within us. We are unaware of our own experiences of deep spiritual wounds, which can show up as physical and mental symptoms, or even when they are obvious and intense, like witnessing horrific scenes of humanitarian tragedies and genocidal wars.

Humanity as a whole yearns for a more soothing, tranquil, and rejuvenating human spirit. In our world, everyday experiences of a degenerate humanity reveal the withered, wretched, and wounded human spirit. Humanity is suffering from an unfathomable spiritual affliction that demands our attention. However, we are naively indifferent. We fail to consider how the spiritual health of our times harms the future of humanity and the planet. We often overlook spiritual health as a crucial aspect of human life, both personally and in social and global contexts. Most importantly, people do not weigh the benefits of spiritual health within the broader scope of human existence.

However, evidence from life also shows that, in many ways, spiritual health is a deep longing and a strong aspiration for everyone. But, at the same time, it is often misunderstood and overlooked. Many people see spiritual and religious phenomena as the same and believe that what happens in religion ensures spiritual health. Ordinary individuals confuse the "religious way of life" with spiritual health or think that becoming religious is the key to achieving it.

Maintaining spiritual health is an endeavor few are willing to invest in and even fewer commit to. Our modern lifestyles constantly challenge our physical and mental well-being. The daily effort to care for one's spiritual health is often overlooked or avoided entirely. Building spiritual health requires effort, time, and self-discipline. The hard work involved in cultivating spiritual health is often less attractive than the quick, ego-boosting benefits of practicing religion.

Spiritual health is essential for human development and a holistic lifestyle. Health sciences focus on spiritual health as a way to improve physical, mental, and social well-being. Human and social sciences highlight that spiritual health significantly influences people's lifestyles, affecting the future of humanity and the planet. Evolutionary sciences are uncovering that spiritual health plays a deterministic role in ongoing evolutionary processes and the next stage of evolution guided by nature.

The spiritual is innate to human nature, and spiritual health is a fundamental human experience. The "spiritual" is an essential part of human life and existence. Neuroscience shows there is a neural basis for spiritual human nature. Neuroscientists have identified a part of the human brain, called the "spiritual brain," that is not found in animals. They provide evidence for the neurobiological roots of spiritual health. This suggests that the "spiritual" cannot be seen as merely cultural, ethereal, or celestial.

What modern sciences reveal is that spiritual health results from the lifelong process of self-evolution and the evolution of human consciousness. It is influenced by the "spiritual brain," not by people's religious beliefs and practices. Evidence from life suggests that, in the way people tend to be human today, the "spiritual brain" is less developed than in past generations. Human life today shows that people are more like automatons, without soul or animation.

The new evolving science of spiritual health has yet to make its mark on ordinary people's thinking. I intend this book to serve as a bird's-eye view of the science of spiritual health. The book deals with spiritual health as a health phenomenon in science, not as a subject matter of theology or religion. It will discuss the neurobiological processes involved in growing spiritual health that will help the reader understand and appreciate the innate spiritual human nature vis-à-vis religious utopias and doctrines.

On an individual level, the potential of innate spiritual human nature is essential for fulfilling human life and enhancing health and happiness. On a collective level, it positively influences society's welfare and the health of humanity. It will help the reader see that the material trajectory of human nature—dominating human life in our world—only partly provides for the "good life." It will demonstrate the broad effects of spiritual health on personal, social, and global well-being, as well as on the health of the planet.

For some, the book could open eyes to aspects of spiritual health that may not have been considered before. It highlights the difference between "religious" and "spiritual" phenomena. It helps readers understand that spiritual health is not about any theological systems, religious beliefs, practices, or spirituality frameworks. It stresses that being correctly guided through life's journey doesn't rely on the utopias of religions or spiritualities. Instead, it relates to understanding human nature, which can either aid or hinder us in developing holistic personhood and a well-rounded way of life—qualities much needed in our world. This book explores spiritual health as a part of holistic health, with implications for individuals, society, humanity, and the planet.

Cultivating spiritual health is closely linked to brain systems, functions, and mechanisms—the neurobiological processes unique to humans. It isn't just about accepting religious doctrines or performing rituals. Doctrinaire religion offers little to no benefits in improving spiritual health, which is a crucial pathway to holistic health, human development, and creating a healthier humanity and a safer world. I hope you will learn from this book the importance, requirements, and benefits of enhancing your spiritual health.

This book examines the human spirit of our times, which is often overlooked when seeking solutions to human problems and global challenges. It highlights humanity's deep spiritual wounds experienced both individually and collectively every day in our world. One may realize that failing to distinguish between religious and spiritual phenomena causes the daily care of spiritual health to be neglected. It offers insights into what modern health sciences are revealing about innate spiritual human nature and spiritual health. Importantly, it presents evidence-based practices, validated by modern health science research, to enhance spiritual health and emphasizes the crucial role of the true self as the guiding principle in human life.

It would be naïve to believe that we can continue living as we do without recognizing that we are surviving human life with a withered, wretched, and wounded human spirit. Everything happening in our world—threatening unimaginable disasters, calamities, catastrophes, and even the annihilation of humanity and the planet—is like a clarion call to awaken to the state of the human spirit within us and the potential of spiritual human nature to positively change the course of human life and focus on growing spiritual health.

Each person's spiritual health impacts the world around them. The overall spiritual well-being of humanity is our only resource for creating a better, safer world—one with a healthier humanity and a thriving planet for future generations.

EXAMINING THE HUMAN SPIRIT OF OUR TIMES

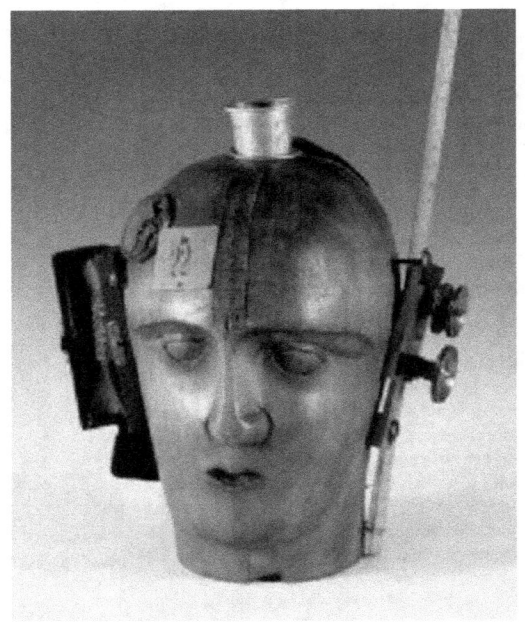

The Spirit of Our Times

Raoul Hausmann (1921) in Los Angeles: Tashen, 2004

This is one of the most well-known works by the German artist Raoul Hausmann. Completed in 1921, the piece is a collection of various common tools and devices attached to a wooden dummy head that is symmetrical and simple. It has no pupils in the eyes, no ears, and no hair. It depicts the human figure without uniqueness or sophistication.

In this wooden dummy, Hausmann illustrated how he perceived the human in the post-WWI era. It shows the human lacking any expression of the human spirit. The title of the piece, Spirit of Our Times, reveals Hausmann's intention. The shape of the human head expresses the view of the post-WWI human as unanimated and drained of spirit.

Human excellence, both individually and collectively, is the result of the human spirit. The spirit influences, guides, and impacts all aspects of human existence. Through the spirit, we transcend our material human nature, distinguishing us from other creatures in the animal kingdom. The spiritual aspect of human nature can positively help us grow and develop human personhood. Individually and together, our health, happiness, and quality of life are driven by the human spirit. Above all, unlike other creatures, we can develop spiritual capacities, making us unique in the animal kingdom.

In a world of material prosperity, like never before in human history, how is the human spirit expressed? In the postmodern era, how does the "technologization" of human life reveal the human spirit? How do digitalization, globalization, ethnopluralism, and culturalism influence the spirit of our time? What inner and outer forces are shaping the human spirit of our world?

These are essential questions to ask if we want to understand the concept of spiritual human nature and spiritual health, and how these phenomena differ from simply being a religious person and the "religious way of life."

There is no denying that the technological environment and materialistic culture play a deterministic role in shaping the human spirit of our times. Today, every person's life is predominantly influenced by the forces of technology and materialism. Human life today is deeply impacted by technology and materialism. The technological and consumerist frameworks in everyday life demonstrate and exert an unstoppable influence on all aspects of human existence. Acquisitive consumption and the technologization of human life are everywhere.

Technology and materialism exert an unrestrained influence and control over all aspects of human existence. No one escapes the effects of modern technology and wealth accumulation. They shape every part of people's daily lives. They influence the relentless global push to deconstruct the "whole" human nature and systematically diminish the spiritual dimension of human life, eroding the spiritual human essence and damaging the human spirit in our times. These global forces of technology and materialism deeply impact the human spirit worldwide.

As difficult as it is to admit, today the spirit of individualism, materialism, and consumerism dominates the human spirit. Excessive desires and insatiable wants are what drive people. Material pursuits focus on external appearances and distract us from non-material aspects of human nature. We are diverted from the inner workings of the mind and the human spirit within us. We often overlook the impact of our human spirit on our way of living and how our lives affect others and the environment.

The pursuit of success focused on possessions is diverting us from the truth about human nature and the vital issues affecting human life. The spirit of individualism, materialism, and consumerism is soul-draining and destroys the essence of human reality. The potential of a renewing and invigorating human spirit for a meaningful life has become like gold dust buried beneath the hunger of the heart.

We face daily challenges in understanding what it means to be human in the postmodern world. We set life goals and create a life orientation that undermines the positive forces of the human spirit. Yet, every day, we also yearn for the spirit to revive and energize us, to fill us with inner freedom, calm, and contentment, and to help us experience greater joy and fulfillment. Modern health science shows that these are essential for holistic health, well-being, and happiness in life.

Today, the human being primarily displays a way of life based on a one-dimensional view of human nature. In the postmodern world, more people live with a skewed and flawed understanding of human nature. The rejection, if not denial, of the spiritual aspect of human nature is deeply unsettling the whole of humanity. This is reflected in the widespread, frantic, restless, miserable, wounded, and vile spirit of our times.

We are experiencing a humanity that is disoriented and caught in the midst of unimaginable consequences. Typically, this manifests through ideological, cultural, and political conflicts. Humanity faces serious existential threats that reveal more about the wounded, suffering human spirit. Our collective humanity lacks the spirit of peace, contentment, and joy. It is evident in a disoriented humanity tightly grasped by overwhelming existential anxiety that refuses to subside.

The material trajectory is steadily shaping a painfully chaotic world. People everywhere are overwhelmed by deep feelings of turmoil, confusion, hatred, hostility, anger, pain, anxiety, and fear, all of which devastate the spirit of freedom, calm, and contentment. The alarming rates of homicide and suicide, illicit drug use, black hat crimes, and the terrible violence, crimes, global terrorism, and many unspeakable evils that are unique to modern society simply reflect the turbulent human spirit of our time.

Only a few believe that the challenges and problems on personal, social, and global levels are caused by the material path of human nature dominating life and weakening the human spirit of our times. Experts argue that everything experienced in human life today, which makes us less than what it means to be human, results from deep spiritual wounds.

Dismissing the spiritual dimension of human life has serious and harmful effects on human existence. Ordinary people endure many difficult and destructive experiences of deep spiritual pain. They feel it daily through intense psychological, emotional, mental health, and physical struggles. This leads to profound turmoil and distress in everyday life. It manifests as social deviation and various other social issues. Experts believe that a wounded human spirit today is a precursor to many physical and mental health problems unique to our era.[1]

In literature, scholars and researchers show that the rise in mental health issues and violence in modern society reflects deep-seated pain. They describe this suffering as spiritual wounding. They present evidence of spiritual wounding affecting all demographics, populations, socio-cultural contexts, life situations, and regions around the world.

Suffering and affliction are unavoidable in human life. However, the kind of human suffering experienced today goes deep into a person's core. There is a profound groan of the human spirit reflected in the intense suffering seen in our world. You can feel the agony of the human spirit in our daily feelings, thoughts, actions, and behaviors. Today, we witness on a global scale the destructive effects of a tormented human spirit.

In health literature, scholars and experts assert that spiritual affliction surpasses all other forms of human suffering. It goes beyond any physical injury, psychological pain, and social affliction. They describe the experience as a relentless feeling of unending suffering, the kind that causes inertia. Those experiencing the condition are usually in denial or ignore it.

The spiritual wounds in modern society often show up in various obsessions, addictions, and acts of violence—and also in many physical, mental, and social health problems. The experience of spiritual wounds in people's daily suffering, pain, and mental stress feels like waves on a beach pulling them out

---

[1] Nonnemaker JM, McNeely CA, Blum RW, Public and Private Domains of Religiosity and Adolescent Health Risk Behaviors: Evidence from the National Longitudinal Study of Adolescent Behaviors. Social science & medicine, December 2003.

from under their feet.

Spiritual affliction is a complex and multifaceted human experience. Its symptoms often involve a clash between our thoughts and emotions, leading to instability and turmoil. Spiritual wounding occurs when a person's sense of self, purpose, and relationships is put at risk, and they remain silent. A key sign of spiritual wounding in our world is that many people have come to accept living without hope, love, and trust as the norm. We've grown numb to the absence of meaning and purpose in life, even when we reflect on our own actions.

Simone Weil, the French philosopher, mystic, social activist, and prolific writer on spiritual wounding, described spiritual affliction as an "uprooting of life, a kind of a death" and "an extreme form of suffering as something apart, unique and irreducible." In her writings, she emphasizes that the essential task of addressing spiritual affliction is to recover the "core of all good" that is shared by all humans. The "core of all good," she references, is the "spiritual component" that is inherent to human nature.[2] The spiritual aspect in humans is like a reservoir of both good and evil. It is about the potential of spiritual human nature to bring about either blessing or ruin in human life.

What is clearly evident from life experiences in our world is that spiritual wounds mainly reveal themselves through psycho-emotional and social imbalances that people face every day. It is most noticeable that the wounded human spirit of our times is widespread and experienced in many ways across our world, yet often denied. Each day, individuals' spiritual suffering deepens the collective spiritual wounds in society.

Trapped in a world of profound human suffering and inhumane cruelty, people are overwhelmed by relentless despair and find no comfort anywhere. Today, the misuse and abuse of prescription medicines, along with illegal drugs and mind-altering substances, show that spiritual wounds are not

---

[2] Simone Weil, <u>Love in the Void: Where God Finds us.</u>(1947) and <u>Oppression and Liberty.</u> (1950) Routledge

receiving the attention they need in daily life.

The spiritual wounds in our world are deeply felt every day through overwhelming feelings of depression and anxiety. The intense sense of inner emptiness, aimlessness, and alienation confuses people in life. Many find themselves drifting and feeling unsettled. Some struggle with understanding life's deeper meaning or even questioning if life truly matters. In literature, spiritual experts argue that today, local, national, and global tensions, conflicts, and hostilities reflect spiritual wounds occurring on a worldwide scale.[3]

Spiritual afflictions negatively impact the moral self of individuals and the overall moral health of humanity. Unclear life purpose and meaning, combined with an unstable sense of self, shape people's lifestyles and relationships, distracting them from spiritual wounds and even making them worse. The surge in deviant moral and social behaviors indicates that people are not giving the spiritual wounds the attention they need.

The current times are often described as marked by profound spiritual suffering. Personally, this manifests in a lifelong history of severe psychological struggles, marginal social and sexual adjustment, self-destructive behaviors, violations of basic human decency, and even health issues. On a societal level, spiritual afflictions frequently hinder efforts toward human solidarity and weaken the fabric of coexistence. Globally, these spiritual struggles are causing many complex existential disruptions. It would be untrue to deny that today there is a widespread sense of spiritual woundedness in human life.

Health professionals and researchers claim that a lack of awareness of the spiritual aspect of human life causes people's suffering to become more intense. They argue that everyday struggles become even more painful, confusing, and destructive. It is unwise to ignore the spiritual part of human nature or dismiss the tensions, conflicts, and pressures caused by the human spirit in our times. There is a collective denial that the modern, soulless human

---

[3] The Dalai Lama on HAPPINESS AND SUFFERING, Braided Way Magazine, August 2018

being and uninspiring humanity are the result of a withered, wounded, and malign human spirit.

Humanity clearly shows a human spirit that is wounded, troubled, chaotic, and desperate for comfort and calm. Truth be told, this is essentially a consequence of polarizing figures on the world stage who are effectively wreaking havoc on ordinary people's human spirit. Fanatical rhetoric promoting extreme ideologies degrades the human spirit of our times. Public officials, influential figures, and powerful members of society cause more harm than good to the human spirit today.

The Buddhist scholar and environmental activist Joanna Macy suggests, "To heal our society, our psyches must heal as well. The military, social, and environmental threats we face do not originate from outside sources; they reflect what's inside us—our fears, greed, and hostilities that split us from ourselves and each other. For our sanity and survival, it's necessary to pursue spiritual and social change, blending the inner with the outer pathways."[4]

The scientific community is starting to focus on the deep spiritual wounds experienced in human life. Healthcare practitioners pay more attention to people's life-orienting systems, the internal changes these cause, and the external events destroying the human from within. Health scientists, ecologists, environmentalists, and everyday citizens worldwide agree that spiritual wounds in our society need urgent attention from everyone.

On a positive note, evolutionary theorists and experts see the spiritual wounds of our times as a sign of the next stage of natural evolution.[5] They argue that the next phase of evolution, as ordained by nature, is the development of humanity's consciousness. They believe this is happening even without our

---

[4] Joanna Macy, World as Lover, World as Self. Parallax Press, 2021
[5] Maynard SJ, Szathmáry E. The Major Transitions in Evolution. Oxford Univ. Press 1995.
Ekstig B. The Pattern of Life. Author House, 2011.
Ekstig B, Complexity, Natural Selection and the Evolution of Life and Humans. PubMed Central, May 2014

awareness. The new, pre-ordained consciousness of humanity is closely linked to the spiritual health of individual people.

Everyone must hear and heed the call for spiritual healing in human life today. It requires all of us to care about and work toward growing spiritual health, not just being a religious person. There is an urgent need for governments, public forums, and both national and international policies, as well as social and health scientists, to pay more attention to experiences of spiritual wounds in the postmodern world. These issues are often ignored when addressing the dilemmas, challenges, and problems we face.

To sum up:

We have become numb to the spiritual side of human life, ignoring spiritual health as a vital part of one's overall health and the well-being of humanity. This has led to a way of being human that has harmful effects on individuals, society, and humanity as a whole. Religion often fails to focus on nurturing the spiritual nature of humans in the postmodern world for the purpose of transforming humanity.

The human spirit of our times reveals much about the false map of human nature that creates perceptual limitations and hampers deeper insight and intuition. Our favored way of life focuses on the external, superficial, and shallow. We ignore the many drawbacks of the acquisitive and hedonistic mindset.

The way to be human in today's world is shaped by technological and cultural determinism. It is creating a human reality unlike any before. The "new" human reality proves to be a harrowing – even shattering – human experience. Striking influencers suggest that the new human phenomenon is having serious consequences for the entire human race.[6] Warnings are sounding about the new

---

[6] Pope John Paul II ADDRESS TO THE 34TH GENERAL ASSEMBLY OF THE UNITED NATIONS, 1979
Gottlieb D, The Wounding and Healing of the Human Spirit. Friends Journal, December 2005

human reality posing a serious threat to the future of humanity and even the destruction of the planet.

The wounded spirit of humanity in today's world shows up as the existential angst of our era. Religious practices, beliefs, pilgrimages, and similar acts do not remove the existential struggles or erase the societal problems caused by people's spiritual wounds. We naively ignore that the chaos and turmoil in the world reflect the chaos and turmoil within individuals and stem from a disturbed human spirit. The most significant human tragedy today is the intrusive cultural influences that cause the wandering, unsettling, and lifeless human spirit in everyone.

The ongoing struggle to incorporate the spiritual dimension of life has been the same throughout human history. It involves the effort to move beyond infectious ideologies, seek clarity and calmness, cope with pathological restlessness heightened by culture, develop and sustain a moral character, and align human consciousness and personal maturity with the existential realities of each era, among many other challenges.

Today, as in past ages, humanity faces a key choice – either to turn suffering into violence and violence into suffering or to convert suffering into healing energy and violence into creative energy in the world. It depends on how we go beyond ourselves. The strength of humanity's spiritual health can only be rooted in transcendence.

We all have the innate ability to go beyond our material human nature. We can move past a self-centered way of life driven by individualism, consumerism, and hedonism. We all need to overcome the "lower self" and connect deeply with the "higher self" of personhood. We must reach out to everything outside ourselves to achieve greater health for humanity, human solidarity, and the world.

The core of our ability to transcend resides in our spiritual human nature, not in religious doctrines or religiosity. It is the only path that guides us toward wisdom, truth, gratitude, hope, beauty, and excellence, and helps us feel more connected to the web of life. Our capacity for transcendence, soulfulness, and holistic living stems from our spiritual health and is vital for renewing the spirit of our times.

A SCIENTIFIC INVESTIGATION INTO SPIRITUAL HUMAN NATURE

In our times, equating machines with humans has come to define our understanding of human nature. Technology causes us to view the human person in terms of the specific operations of machines. Technological capabilities have been shown to be no different from human capacities. Technology even demonstrates the ability to surpass what humans are able to do.

As nearly all aspects of human life become adapted to the technologization of human existence, we are steadily moving along the material path toward the denial of the spiritual dimension of human life. This material trajectory shapes everyday human psychology and behaviors. The omnipresence of technology and cyberspace clearly marks the cultural peak of this trajectory.

Furthermore, modern technological advances have created enormous "material excesses." No one can avoid being surrounded by an abundance of material goods and services. We are constantly pushed to have more, accomplish more, and accumulate more. We don't know any other way to live. Our materialistic pursuits and goals have become uncontrollable, often blinding us to the spiritual side of life.

The "technologization" of human existence and "material excesses" have woefully led to the existential fallacy about what truly makes up human nature. We tend to think and live as if only the material aspects define human nature. This material view becomes ingrained with each passing day. We live with a one-dimensional understanding of human nature.

What is the model of our human nature – the material or non-material – that we use to understand ourselves and others? Does human nature have a spiritual component, and importantly, in the technological world, does it go beyond technologization? What model of human nature – the material or non-material – guides our daily thoughts, feelings, actions, and behaviors? How accurate or inaccurate is the map? How is it working for us? These are pressing questions for us to explore regarding spiritual human nature and the cultivation of spiritual health.

Understanding human nature—our own nature—is essential to shaping human life and existence. The opposite—failing to understand ourselves—clearly leads to existential issues. Understanding one's human nature is not some lofty, abstract intellectual exercise. It comes down to a simple question: Why do we do what we do?

We already have our own answers and live the way we do. These answers, whether good or bad, form the map of human nature we carry around every day. It is the CPU of our lives. It contains the core ideas that guide much of what we do, think, feel, perceive, believe, and experience in life.

To survive the years between birth and death, we all must navigate the terrain of human life in this world. Throughout our lives, we grope across a rugged landscape filled with struggles, challenges, and problems. The span of a human life is a demanding and strenuous journey. Without the proper map of human nature – even one that's slightly inaccurate or incomplete – we risk ending up in some form of existential quicksand.

The tragic events in the postmodern world indicate that an incorrect view of human nature is preventing proper and effective solutions to challenges, struggles, and problems in human life. The way we live today shows that we are naive to think our human life and existence can survive without spiritual human nature.

In our times, enlightened world leaders, global experts, pundits, and the scientific community, when highlighting the many unique dilemmas, challenges, and problems facing humanity in the postmodern world, suggest that these issues are related to people's understanding of human nature. It is clear and noticeable that the material aspect of human nature largely influences how we live today.

Usually, we think of human nature only in terms of the physical or material aspects, but human nature isn't just about the biological body. The spirit is an integral part of human nature. Like the body and mind, the spirit is fundamental to human nature at all times and in all places. The "whole" human nature includes the body, mind, and spirit.

No one is alive with only a body or without the mind and spirit. The spirit is essential to human existence, just like the body. You might say the mind and spirit are like wings that enable the physical body to travel through space and time. The material and non-material aspects of human nature are never separate, even though they are distinct components.

Normal human nature unites and synthesizes both material and non-material components. These elements are fundamental to the human phenomenon. The entire human experience comprises these two components of human nature, which inherently define human personhood.

The human species, like everything in the natural world, shares in organic matter. However, while part of the natural world, humans can transcend their organic nature through intellectual, spiritual, and moral capacities. The spiritual aspect of human nature is not some existential mystery. It is present in everything that makes human nature different from animal nature. The spiritual sets humans apart from the rest of the animal kingdom.

The spiritual is an experiential, existential human phenomenon that makes the human species both unique and distinct in the natural world. As humans, we all sense that there is something more about our human nature, cr at least the potential for something more. We use words like "soul," "spirit," "nous," "Atman," "Self," "Buddha nature," "Imago Dei," and similar terms to highlight the innate spiritual aspect of human nature.

The idea that there is more to our human nature distinguishes the "non-physical' aspect of humans from the rest of nature. Every form of human expression and manifestation testifies to this. The spiritual not only elevates human nature within the animal kingdom but also makes it crucial to human development, health, and all aspects of life. The Psalmist in the Bible expressed this well when he viewed humans as a little less than the gods.[7] He didn't see humans as merely animals.

The experience of something more profound about our human nature points to a capacity that is independent of external conditions. It is an innate ability, not merely a stimulus-triggered phenomenon. It goes beyond physical sensory comfort. What modern science reveals is that humans have a uniquely evolved neurobiology that supports our spiritual human nature. This stems from the inherent brain mechanisms in humans. It is the innate potential humans possess to animate and energize or weaken and deplete human life.

We express the spiritual nature of human beings through everyday life events and situations. The human spirit can be a positive or negative force within a person. It has the power to bring blessings or cause destruction. The spirit in a person can either help them succeed or lead to their downfall. It can turn life's toughest challenges into tremendous opportunities, or it can cause a person's life to fall apart. The spirit can lay the groundwork for health, happiness, and fulfillment, or it can become an obstacle. The power of human spiritual nature in the "world" of humans is beyond imagination.

The human spirit influences all of humanity, not just the individual. It helps to shape and sometimes destroy society and humankind. A healthy society and humanity are reflected in the regenerative powers of the human spirit that

---

[7] Psalm 8:5

invigorate everyone. Striving for human excellence is both a personal and collective effort of the human spirit. Every day, the human spirit creates happiness and health, or their opposites, on personal, social, and global levels.

Today, many of humanity's problems and threats to our planet are mainly caused by the corrupted human spirit. We see this spirit every day through ongoing existential struggles and issues. We live in a world driven by the material side of human nature. We distort and devalue the spiritual side of life. We embrace and participate in a culture that pulls us away from developing spiritual health, leaving it an unused resource in human life.

The material aspect of human nature is overstated in the postmodern world, often cloaked in scientific language. Science claims that everything about being human is based on the material. The human being is defined and understood through the unique organization and function of material parts. Modern science has explained many aspects of our material nature and aims to explain the rest in the future. Will it actually succeed? Or is this idea a sign of science's limitations?

What we know about modern science is that it has not been able to fully explain the different levels of human experience. It does not differentiate between the intangible non-material aspects of human reality and the physical or biological parts. The non-material aspects of human existence aren't highlighted in science. Science tends to avoid the spiritual side of human life or only speculates about this part of our existence.

So far, the scrutiny and investigation of modern science into the spiritual aspect of human nature are lacking in substance. Scientific research provides an insufficient explanation for the beneficial and harmful effects of the spiritual component of human nature. Although neuroscience has advanced in helping us better understand how the "spiritual brain" plays a crucial role in human spirituality, some argue it is nothing more than a materialist view of human nature.[8]

However, an average person experiences spiritual human nature as a normal part of life. It is a common human phenomenon that influences how we live. It becomes clearly visible in daily life through our actions as humans. Every aspect of human existence reflects the influence of the human spirit, whether it is regenerative or degenerative.

The human spirit manifests differently in various people and situations. It has a certain quality that can be either uplifting and energizing or weakening and disastrous, even terrifying and destructive, in both individuals and organizations. It is a personal experiential phenomenon that greatly influences daily human life and existence.

When people recognize the "spiritual" part within themselves, they also understand the phenomenon as a practical, straightforward, transformative reality. The phenomenon is a clear and fundamental aspect of existence. There is no need for logical reasoning or scientific explanation about it. It is experienced through the physical and/or mental human reality it creates for individuals at any given moment. The map of human nature that includes the "spiritual" helps them develop a mindset to understand human life differently than without it.

Mapping the journey of life with one's spiritual nature is not about dealing with likelihood and probability, but about seeking absolute certainty. It involves developing sense perceptions, instincts, and intuitions to navigate more deliberately, intelligently, and effectively through the rugged terrain of human life. It does not oppose but instead deepens the experience of all aspects of human nature. The spiritual human nature has the potential to make the journey through the challenging landscape of human existence less exhausting. It plays a crucial role in helping people manage existential struggles more effectively.

---

[8] Editorial, <u>Does Neuroscience Threaten Human Values?</u> Nature (1) 1998

To better understand the inherent spiritual human nature, we will analyze the neurobiological processes involved in its development. This analysis will focus on two areas: (1) "exceptional spiritual experiences" and (2) human consciousness.

"Exceptional Spiritual Experiences"

Humans are inherently embodied spiritual beings capable of experiencing non-ordinary creaturely states. We all encounter such experiences, which research literature calls "exceptional spiritual experiences." Health scientists and experts argue that these experiences are similar to everyday feelings like joy, peace, wonder, love, and the like.

The phenomenon of "exceptional spiritual experiences" is fundamental to what it means to be human. Every day non-ordinary human experiences – "exceptional spiritual experiences" – consistently affirm the spiritual nature of humans. Neuroscience is beginning to show that the "exceptional spiritual experiences" phenomenon can be observed in the neurobiological processes of the human mind.[9]

Researchers in neuroscience and psychology demonstrate that the human brain systems and mechanisms can lead to "exceptional spiritual experiences." They show that these experiences are not always religious. They can occur during everyday moments like being close to someone, walking in the woods, reading a book, or watching a movie. Health research provides evidence of the firm and lasting positive effects of "exceptional spiritual experiences" on people's mental and physical health.[10]

Scientists have demonstrated that neurobiological processes are involved in all of our normal and extraordinary human experiences, as well as our responses and lessons learned from them. Essentially, the entire scope of

---

[9] Newberg A, Principles of Neurotheology. Routledge Science and Religion, 2017
[10] Puchalski, C. M., The role of spirituality in health care. Baylor University Medical Center Proceedings (Vol 14), 2001
Long, Katelyn N G, et.al. Spirituality As A Determinant Of Health: Emerging Policies, Practices, And Systems. Health Affairs (Vol 43), 2024

human nature involves the functions of the human brain. The ordinary human organism becomes extraordinary through brain activity. The human brain systems influence the aspect of non-material human nature.

There is a consensus in contemporary neuroscience that whatever the relationships are between "spiritual realities" and the material world, they are mediated through the brain. Neuroscience emphasizes that altered neural pathways lead to "exceptional spiritual experiences," which are unique to human existence.

Neuroscientists have identified that the neurological processes underlying the "exceptional spiritual experience" are a result of neurochemistry and neuroplasticity. Neuroscience provides evidence showing that the brain chemicals and plasticity cause changes in the cognitive and affective regions of the brain during "exceptional spiritual experiences."[11]

Sometimes, the "exceptional spiritual experiences" evoke a sense of the transcendental dimension of human life. The phenomenon in individuals indicates that humans are inherently capable of transcending the creaturely limits known in the natural world. The power of the human spirit is clearly shown through human abilities to go beyond the material aspects of human nature.

Typically, these are capacities that help the human mind to abstract, reason, and seek the truth on a deeper level of human intelligence. On the level of the human will, it emphasizes that we are endowed with inherent abilities to freely self-determine and act in pursuit of the most relevant and purposeful goals, which serve the common good. Through the human capacity to transcend, we aim for the best interests of all to unify and build a shared humanity.

In health literature, transcendence refers to moving beyond the concrete and physical and connecting with realities outside oneself.

---

[11] Kang Y, Cooper N, Pandey P et.al Effects of Self-Transcendence on Neural Responses to Persuasive Messages and Health Behavior Change. PubMed Central, October 2018

Transcendence is the human ability to forge connections to the larger universe and find meaning beyond oneself. It results from human brain mechanisms that determine spiritual nature and is influenced by the regenerative human spirit.

Human consciousness

What neuroscientists and researchers are indicating is that the human capacity for transcendence is an inherent neurobiological potential. No other species in the animal kingdom can achieve the same level of consciousness for transcendence. The functionality of the human brain network creates consciousness in humans. The experience of transcendence is produced by the brain's cognitive system and processes. Neuroscience shows that anyone can develop transcendence.

To this end, experts argue that the human capacity for transcendence, rooted in spiritual human nature, is a power to rebuild and renew humanity. Without the power of transcendence, we are prone to destroying and ruining ourselves.

The documented evidence shows that the capacity for transcendence provides intuitions, deeper insights, better perceptions, and instinctual wisdom to connect with others, humanity, and the universe. When transcendence is developed in a person, one is able to understand reality without limits and freely direct oneself toward the absolute good.

Transcendence is fundamental to the evolution of human consciousness, which is essential for the development of personhood. Spiritual health is cultivated when "exceptional spiritual experiences" enhance and reinforce the human capacity for transcendence. Lower levels of human consciousness indicate a diminished capacity for transcendence. The health of society and humanity, along with the benefits they provide to the planet, depends on the human capacity for transcendence.

Through the evolution of human consciousness, transcendence serves as the pathway to self-evolution, which is always tied to people's spiritual health. The development of human consciousness and self-evolution are essential to human growth, well-being, and the fulfillment of life. It is the pathway to spiritual health and more meaningful human existence.

Neuroscience shows there is a neural basis for human consciousness. The scientists present evidence for the neurobiological processes involved in human consciousness. Neuroscience emphasizes the human brain as both the receiver and transmitter of human consciousness. Neuroscientists have demonstrated that neurological processes and endocrine systems work together to coordinate, regulate, and produce higher levels of human consciousness.

The human brain can respond to both positive and negative life influences in many different ways. What neuroscience is clear about is that we have the ability to willfully change brain functions to influence consciousness. The human brain can be trained to operate in a way that supports intentional and purposeful living. The potential of human brain systems to develop human consciousness gives a person the ability to reorient themselves in the world.

Scientists utilizing neuroimaging techniques, including functional magnetic resonance imaging, single photon emission computed tomography, and positron emission tomography, have shed light on the neurobiological mechanisms linked to "exceptional spiritual experiences." Neuroscientific discoveries about human neurobiology and neurochemistry have expanded the understanding of the connection between the human brain and spiritual human nature.[12]

What neuroscience is showing us today is that there is constant "becoming" encoded in the human brain through synaptic activity. Humans can sculpt the brain (and thus shape the mind). Both the regenerating and degenerating human are constantly formed from within. This is about the power of the human brain affecting the "spiritual" dimension of human nature.

The brain's neuroplasticity is key to human life processes and experiences. The term 'neuroplasticity' describes the brain's ability to change its

---

[12] Kircher T, David A, The Self in Neuroscience and Psychiatry. Cambridge University Press 2003

function and even structure in response to a person's life experiences, whether mental, physical, or spiritual. Through its plasticity, the human brain influences daily experiences and shapes how we respond to them. Researchers studying brain plasticity have shown there is a reciprocal relationship between the brain's cognitive control and what guides people's daily experiences and behaviors, namely, the human spirit.[13]

Neuroplasticity researchers emphasize not only the importance of the brain in shaping human experience but also the inherent ability humans have to direct their interactions with the world. The human brain enables us to be self-directed in our choices and actions. It provides us with the capacity to exercise a will that is free from external influences.

In the health literature, experts argue that the "spiritual" is a fundamental life principle at the core of the human experience and essential to human health and development. The spiritual aspect of human nature becomes crucial in the context of "exceptional spiritual experiences" and spiritual health. By including the spiritual in our understanding of human nature, we foster the innate abilities for deeper awareness, insight, intuition, psycho-emotional significance, and vibrancy in life. This kind of experience is truly possible only when the whole of human nature guides a person's life path.

In an existential sense, human spiritual nature characterizes all of human existence. It is equivalent to what is essential to human life itself. In this way, the spiritual is a fundamental human phenomenon, and similarly, the experience of spiritual health represents an existential health phenomenon. What is existential is also universal and must be recognized as belonging to all people at all times and in all places.

The human experience depends heavily on the positive effects and benefits of spiritual health in shaping what is truly essential to human life. When addressing the broad range of existential challenges and issues facing humanity

---

[13] Fuchs E, Flugge G, Adult Neuroplasticity: More than 40 Years of Research. PubMed Central, May 2014

today, it centers on the core spiritual health concerns that confront us. This highlights the serious consequences of neglecting spiritual human nature, which has been removed from the understanding of what guides us as humans.

A more holistic understanding of human nature must rely on system-oriented views of the body-mind/brain-spirit and environment connection.

To sum up:

Every tragedy and calamity occurring in our world today reveals a one-dimensional view of human nature guiding people's lives.

Health sciences consider "exceptional spiritual experiences" as ways to enhance and reach a peak in spiritual health. They highlight that spiritual health involves a lifelong process of evolving consciousness and self-development.

Research scientists have shown that the spiritual aspect of health is a practical concept that should be developed throughout a person's life. They also emphasize that everyone's spiritual health is closely connected to the well-being of humanity. It is nurtured by achieving "wholeness" and embracing a "wholesome" lifestyle.[14]

The fundamental human nature forms the foundation of spiritual human nature, regardless of religion. Neuroscience is beginning to show that spiritual human nature is a real bio-psycho-social potential in humans. It is an innate ability that influences human health, life, and existence.

Neurobiological and psychological sciences reveal that human nature is "charged" with the presence of the "spiritual." The constant change of the brain is normal, inherent, and occurs regardless of human intention or awareness. Brain-related sciences provide us with invaluable insights into the spiritual aspects of human nature. The neurobiology of humans has the ability to expand the cognitive domain for "exceptional spiritual experiences."

The "whole" human reality is only experienced by the "whole" human

---

[14] Fisher JW, <u>Understanding and Assessing Spiritual Health.</u> International Handbook of Education for Spirituality, Care and Wellbeing, January 2009

nature. The material and non-material aspects make up the "whole" human nature. The "whole" human reality appears through the harmonious functioning of body, mind, spirit, and environment. The entire human person is shaped by both nature and nurture. The core of the human person includes the capacity for transcendence and consciousness.

In modern society, people seem blind to human virtues, high-mindedness, higher purposes, integrity, and character. Neither is the best version of oneself nor the shining life one can develop ever completely within reach. We spend years of life just surviving without truly living. Without the positive benefits generated from spiritual human nature, people's lives are deeply affected in a harmful way.

EXAMINING THE RELIGIOUS AND SPIRITUAL PHENOMENA

In a scientifically rational world, the biggest obstacle to spiritual health and well-being is the confusion between "spiritual" and "religious." People often view the two as equivalent, partly due to their strong historical connection. This makes it easy to use the terms interchangeably. As a result, spiritual health is frequently associated with having a religious faith and religiosity. Furthermore, with the growth of a "spiritual marketplace," following a specific spiritual cult or adopting a particular spiritual system is usually seen as a way to achieve spiritual health.

The spiritual and religious phenomena overlap in many ways, but they are neither the same nor completely opposite. Both the spiritual and religious worldviews rely on humans' inherent spiritual nature. Both seek to reveal the potential inherent in human spiritual nature. Both involve metaphysical realities and ontological experiences. Both highlight the transcendental dimension of human life and emphasize higher ideals and purposes. Both promote virtues like love, forgiveness, compassion, peace, hope, and humility, and they work toward the common good. Both emphasize personal integrity, moral values, and ethical behavior, focusing on reverence for human life, respect for human rights, and building a more compassionate world. Essentially, both aim to cultivate the sublime aspects of human nature.

Although they overlap, there are differences. The main difference is that religion is learned, while the "spiritual" is innate. Unlike religion, the spiritual is a core part of human nature, just like the mind and body are. The "religious" is learned through belief systems, rules, and rituals, but the "spiritual" is inherent to human nature. Like the mind and body, it is essential to human life and existence.

Religion influences how people think, feel, and act according to a certain way of life, and this is what it means to be "spiritual." However, technically, someone can still experience the spiritual even without religion. Every person, whether they follow a religion or not, is connected to the spiritual. While religion can be changed, replaced, or even abandoned, the spiritual remains a constant, limitless, and eternal human phenomenon.

In the realm of religion, the concept of "spiritual" refers to things beyond the physical world. It's a non-physical force linked to the ethereal and heavenly. However, when viewed through a scientific lens, the "spiritual" becomes a natural part of human experience – a fundamental aspect of our normal human nature. It's a basic, life-giving force that plays a crucial role in human life and existence. At its core, the "spiritual" is a fundamental part of human nature, not something added on by a specific religion, culture, or society.

Most people assume that belonging to a religion is the measure of spiritual health. They don't always realize that there are significant differences between the "religious experience" and the "spiritual experience." These two concepts are often confused in ordinary people's thinking. There is a common misunderstanding of what spiritual health truly involves. Many believe that spiritual health is achieved simply by following religious doctrines, rituals, and observances. This often leads to the misconception that spiritual health is synonymous with religiosity.

Although many people nowadays recognize the distinction between religious and spiritual phenomena, few acknowledge that a "religious experience" is a subjective experience shaped by the framework of religion. In contrast, a "spiritual experience" is not just a subjective experience, limited to a framework, but an objective, boundless phenomenon. The "spiritual experience" cannot be confined to the domain of religion. Unlike the "religious experience," it occurs in a wide range of contexts, even in what religion considers mundane and temporal. The "spiritual experience" is a scientifically objectifiable phenomenon.

Religiosity is rooted in the framework of religion, but spiritual health is based on neurobiological processes. Modern science is revealing the neural basis of the "spiritual experience," distinguishing it from the "religious experience." Neuroscientists and researchers study "spiritual experience" as influenced by brain mechanisms and chemistry. Neuroscience provides evidence that it is an objectifiable human phenomenon.

As a real-life experience, the "spiritual experience" is a fundamental part of being human and is essential for spiritual health and growth. We cannot separate the spiritual from being human, as the possibility exists with religion. Whether or not a person's "religious experience" leads to a "spiritual experience" is a different matter.

A person's religiosity stems from accepting belief systems and rules and participating in ritual practices. In contrast, according to health sciences, spiritual health originates from the core reality of personhood. It concerns the inherent human powers within the true self, which are developed through the evolution of human consciousness and self-evolution.

Spiritual health develops throughout a person's life. It advances by exploring new levels of human consciousness for personal growth. It involves working to become a better version of oneself and seeking a more meaningful human experience through the evolution of consciousness and self-improvement. It results from reaching the peaks of self-transcendence and shows in a deep sense of oneness with all and the universe. In contrast, religion encourages a person to focus on "receiving grace" and being right with God and the world, emphasizing self-attention through growing in "holiness," which is regarded as having spiritual well-being.

Spiritual health differs from religiousness because it is guided by the "inner-core" reality of the person, unveiling the true self and contrasting it with the pseudo-self. This expands the potential for transcendence within the individual, expressed through higher-order personhood – the "higher self." The higher order of personhood is best illustrated by the holistic self, the pursuit of life's higher ideals and purposes, and a sense of humanity that is not overshadowed by remnants of the primitive past.

The inner-core reality of a person has powers that shape or damage one's personhood. It always appears in the active processes of the mind, influencing who one is, could be, or should aim to become. Growing spiritual health is the work done on the inner-core reality through active attention to the mind's processes, which are constantly happening in every moment of life. The effort involved in building spiritual health focuses on being true to the real self as life unfolds.

It must be pointed out that, although the growth of spiritual health in the "religious way of life" may be limited, for many people, it remains the only resource—better than nothing at all—to access the spiritual nature of humanity and engage with life through the innate sense of the spiritual dimension of life. And, although people are generally satisfied with the "spiritual experience" they get from the "religious way of life," which is minimal, evidence shows that religion actually distracts them from their inner core reality, being true to the real self and the higher-order personhood.

The present moment of everyday human life serves as the foundation for building and strengthening our spiritual health. By paying attention to real-life experiences, we stay connected to the true aspects of our personhood and authentic selves. As we progress along the spiritual path, we engage in lifelong processes of "renewing," "becoming," and creating a sense of freshness in our identity.

When this happens, we don't conform to familiar or new molds to pretend who we are or who we are not. The daily experiences of disintegrating personhood are not denied or suppressed but are worked on to create the "wholesomeness" of personhood—the holistic self. People growing in spiritual health recognize that an evolving personhood is unfolding. They have a sense of self that is always a new discovery.

In contrast, in the religious way of life, there is a sense of self that is shaped by the framework of religion and remains static for self-validation. In religion, people aim to be someone other than who they truly are. The individual relies on the acquired "religious selfhood" for self-identity and self-worth. As a result, the thinking patterns developed through religion greatly influence how they treat themselves and others. This is often experienced as hypercritical attitudes, harsh judgments, and pharisaical tendencies.

Critics of religion argue that it burdens the mind with "dos" and "don'ts." They claim that the controls and rules silently enforced in religion effectively hinder people's self-awareness and the realities of life as they unfold. In the "religious way of life," loyalty to doctrines, rituals, and rules takes priority over who the person truly is or what they think and experience.

In religion, the theological utopias and doctrinal beliefs draw people's attention away from life as it happens in the present. Religion distracts individuals from the ongoing processes of the mind, the complex inner-core reality, and the true self of a person. Few recognize the "religious way of life" as alienating them from their true self and creating a divide between the real self and life as it occurs in real-time experiences.

The primary objective of spiritual health development is to facilitate self-evolution, personal growth, psychosocial maturity, and holistic living. It involves becoming an instrument of change in the world without forcing theories and methods of change. This can only happen while a person is alive and in self-renewal mode. When the focus is on cultivating spiritual health, people aim to become a better version of themselves in the present moment and support the cause of a healthier humanity. Each individual recognizes their personhood as the channel to build human solidarity without excluding anyone, creating a better world, and fostering a healthier society.

This starkly contrasts the cultivation of spiritual health with the "religious way of life." Like any other industry, religion promotes a product—an afterlife offering—such as heaven, salvation, redemption, liberation, moksha, and similar concepts. The focus in human life shifts to what happens after death, not during life. The goal of human existence is otherworldly and not aligned with real life as it occurs.

Modern critics of religion argue that human life, while lived, does not receive as much attention as the rewards or punishments in the afterlife. This is because the primary focus of religion is not on who a person truly is or can be while alive. In the "religious way of life," the emphasis is on what happens after death rather than on everyday life processes. When religion dominates a person's life, the afterlife becomes an obsession, shifting focus away from living in the present and the ongoing experience of life.

Religion confines people within mental boundaries, and the "religious way of life" seeks to make individuals conform to the framework of religion. Within this religious framework, doctrinal schemas define human nature and determine what is considered the infinite value of human worth. Religion makes claims about the indefinable human value that undermine the entire human phenomenon. However, the phenomena of human personhood transcend the doctrinal boundaries of religion.

Some social scientists observe that significant distortions in human worth result from linking self-cognition and self-identity with religious doctrines.[15] They believe that religious teachings often promote unhealthy views of human nature and foster negative perceptions and attitudes toward human life. They highlight that combining legal and theological systems to

---

[15] Baker JO. & Whitehead AL, Homosexuality, Religion and Science: Moral Authority and the Persistence of Negative Attitudes. Sociological Inquiry; 2012.

define human worth actually leads to experiences of unstable selfhood and fluid self-identity in individuals. They criticize religion for making claims about the infinite and unquantifiable value of human beings.

The primary purpose of human life is to become whole. A holistic person includes the entire human experience—mind, body, spirit, genetics, and environment. The "religious way of life" aims at growing in "holiness," not holistically. The idea of holiness emphasizes piety, devotion, and duty to religious practices, whereas holism focuses on becoming a complete human being. It involves continuous efforts toward "self-integration," "self-coherency," and "self-consistency." Life teaches us that maintaining a wholesome personhood depends on nurturing spiritual health, not just accepting doctrines.

Anthropologically and psychologically, the holistic human person results from the evolution of human consciousness and self-development. It is the effort made daily to piece together the fragmented parts of oneself and to develop all-encompassing life perspectives that are inclusive, responsible, and humane.

In striving for holiness, people often balance unresolved psychological and emotional issues with loyalty to religious beliefs, ideals, and groups—the framework of religion for the sense of self can limit personal growth and maturity. Unlike the "holy" person, the holistic person pursues psychosocial maturity, emphasizes belonging to the web of life, values equality and fairness, and develops human solidarity with all, saints and sinners.

As a person becomes more "whole," they develop a holistic approach to life centered on balance and harmony. This involves understanding how every aspect of a person—physical, emotional, mental, social, spiritual, and moral—is interconnected. A holistic way of life isn't about being perfect but about embracing the divine-human blend in every aspect of life. Often, this is hindered by religious ideals, practices, and behaviors that emphasize loyalty to doctrine and the concept of a holy person.

Experientially, human growth and maturity culminate in holism and are the most crucial factors in improving human life. Spiritual health is focused on holism—that is, becoming a holistic person, developing holistic health, and living holistically. In health literature, the key goal of all human development and self-improvement is to cultivate a holistic personhood. Psychosocial maturity in individuals reflects holistic personhood and is considered vital for contributing positively to the welfare of society and humanity.

Modern health sciences assert that "spiritual health" is a key pathway to overall well-being and is essential for a holistic lifestyle. The "religious way of life" does not necessarily require someone to be a holistic person, develop holistic health, or adopt a holistic approach. In fact, the rigidity often found in religions can create worldviews that conflict with what is needed to foster holism. Health science literature highlights many adverse effects that religion can have on individuals' holistic health and lifestyle.

In today's world, there is an undeniable urgency for people to focus on holism. The idea of a holistic person and a holistic way of life is not just about personal well-being but also involves society's welfare. Modern critics of religion argue that religious utopias distract people from holistic growth and living. They contend that without prioritizing or emphasizing the need for human growth, development, and maturity, religion can undermine the goal of holism in human life. Ordinary people often see "doing" religion as an easy way to avoid the hard work of developing holistic personhood and a balanced way of life.

When someone is truly "whole" and "wholesome" in life, there is no denying their authentic self. The inner core reality and true self come to the forefront of awareness. The individual becomes more intentional in self-growth. Their way of being and living, driven by an inner sense of control, shapes their actions. Life orientation and goals show that the "eschaton mentality" does not define how to be human or how to live. They remain deeply connected to real-time human experiences related to everyday life. People seeking spiritual health aim to improve their earthly life while maintaining an outward focus on others and developing relevant skills and behaviors, enhancing the quality of human life for all. The phenomenon of spiritual health is best experienced through the holistic development of a person, providing therapeutic benefits to humanity and the world.

In the animal kingdom, the human species is uniquely endowed with "spiritual capacities." This is a gift of natural evolution. The development of the human brain's systems, functions, and mechanisms has given us a spiritual nature that allows us to rise above the instincts of our primitive ancestors. Scientific evidence shows that the "spiritual" aspect of human nature has a neural basis and can unlock spiritual capacities that are unique to humans.

As humans, we're born with spiritual capacities that transcend the limits of specific religious teachings. However, traditional religion often fails to nurture these inherent spiritual abilities, which are crucial for living a holistic life. Developing spiritual health is essentially about finding balance and completeness in life. Human evolution is designed to help people grow, mature, and evolve over the life span.

Religious practices often overlook or downplay holistic approaches to human growth, psychosocial maturity, and overall well-being. Unlike the development of spiritual health, the idea of the "whole" person and a "wholesome" way of life is neither emphasized nor explored in religion. As a result, people following a "religious way of life" may become desensitized to their own spiritual capacities, which are vital for becoming a well-rounded individual and living a balanced life.

Our ultimate goal in growing spiritually healthy is to cultivate a well-rounded person and way of life. Building spiritual health is a path to holism — to develop a holistic sense of self and live a holistic lifestyle. This involves a deliberate effort to renew ourselves and become our best selves, taking a comprehensive and multi-faceted approach to self-renewal and human transformation.

In health literature, "renewing," "becoming," "wholeness," and "wholesomeness" are the constructs on which spiritual health is built. Experts argue that religions distract people from self-evolution – the lifelong processes of "renewing" and "becoming."[16]

Spiritual health is closely tied to life as it unfolds in the present. In religion, theological ideals, religious dogmas, and "other-worldly aspirations" take precedence over real-time processes of human life and do little to benefit the experience of holism.

Although religion is often seen as ineffective in promoting comprehensive human development and bettering humanity, sociological researchers emphasize that the "religious way of life" fulfills many critical human needs.[17] They argue that religion provides people with community, identity, and psycho-emotional stability, which support fundamental human needs for belonging, self-acceptance, and protection from internal threats. When these needs are satisfied, individuals tend to experience good health. Some misinterpret these positive effects of religion as equivalent to spiritual health.

On the other hand, some argue that religious ideas and beliefs can create a kind of cognitive dissonance in people, which adversely impacts their health. These researchers suggest that this happens because people place a lot of importance on the framework of their religion. The established religious norms can shape how people see their own worth and value. As a result, the value people give to their religious teachings can influence their daily thought patterns, which in turn affect how they treat themselves and others.[18]

When it comes to living a "religious way of life," self-identity and self-

---

[16] Kaku M. The Future of the Mind: The Scientific Quest to Understand, Enhance, and Empower the Mind. Doubleday 2014.

[17] Emerson, MO, Monahan, SC, & Mirola, WA, Religion Matters: What Sociology Teaches Us about Religion in Our World. Upper Saddle River, 2011.

[18] Burris C, Harmon-Jones E, and Tarpley WR, By Faith Slone: Religious Agitation and Cognitive Dissonance. Basic and Applied Social Psychology (19), 1997.

esteem are closely linked to the self-expectations shaped by religion. This is rooted in the strict rules of religious doctrine. But when people prioritize spiritual growth, they develop an "aspirational" sense of self. This self-identity evolves and becomes more complex over time, and it highlights the value of each person in the interconnected web of life.

Although the "aspirational" self-identity is elusive, psychological research shows that it provides more profound and more effective therapeutic benefits for the individual.[19] When people distinguish being religious from developing spiritual health, they concentrate on a self-identity that exists in the present—not the past or future—and that is constantly evolving.

The tangible experience of developing spiritual health is the evolving sense of self influenced by the changing human consciousness. The self-integration processes driven by the evolution of human consciousness expand self-perspectives and foster the experience of unconditional acceptance of oneself and others.

The commitment to self-integration processes highlights the integrity of an individual's self-identity. This serves as the foundation for a person's sense of identity, self-esteem, and engagement in life. Religion reinforces the integrity of self-identity by aligning with doctrinal schemas.

Modern-day critics argue that the constant emphasis on human fallibility and imperfections in religion undermines the self-evolution processes in people.[20] They maintain that the framework of religion makes individuals self-alienated, leading them to lose touch with the "as-is" self-reality. In the "religious way of life," self-acceptance and self-worth are linked to being faithful and loyal to the teachings, rules, and practices of religion. The critics emphasize that all religion does is blind people to their true selves, impair the

---

[19] Burke P J, Stets JE, <u>Identity Theory.</u> Oxford University Press; 2009.
Callero P, <u>Role-Identity Salience.</u> Social Psychology Quarterly (Vol. V) 1985.
[20] Exline JJ, Rose ED, <u>Religious And Spiritual Struggle.</u> Handbook of the Psychology of Religion and Spirituality, 2nd ed. The Guilford Press, 2013.

"whole" human reality in a person, and obstruct the development of the holistic human person.

Researchers have examined the connection between religion and health. In just the first decade of the new millennium, there have been over two thousand such studies. While some researchers highlight the positive effects of the "religious way of life," many suggest that religion can also lead to negative emotional states in people.[21] Some focus on the beneficial influence of religion on mental and physical health, while others point out the adverse effects. In the research literature, criminal behavior, social deviance, and violent or abnormal conduct—such as what is seen in cultural conflicts, communal tensions, ethnic cleansing, and global terrorism—are linked to the psycho-emotional and intellectual restrictions imposed by religion. Religious teachings are known to influence deviant, violent, and immoral behaviors.

According to a 2010 global poll, the majority of people from developed and developing countries believed that religion fosters intolerance, deepens divisions, and hinders progress. Overall, religion was seen in a negative light, with many people feeling that it leads to pessimistic attitudes toward life, society, and the world, as well as mistrust in others.

Researchers have found that societies with healthier populations tend to be less religious.[22] They point to religious ideologies that are used to promote and sustain prejudice, bigotry, hate, and division. Today, we see that absolute religious ideals can lead people to fanaticism and make the world more complicated. However, not many are willing to acknowledge that what is done in religion can keep the human mind in the darkness of ignorance.

---

[21] Religions Wiki website
Baetz M, Bowen R, Jones G, Koru-Sengul T, How Spiritual Values and Worship Attendance Relate to Psychiatric Disorders in the Canadian Population. Canadian Journal of Psychiatry, 2006
[22] Cruz M, Pincus HA, Welsh DE, Greenwald S, Lasky E, Kilbourne AM, The Relationship between Religious Involvement and Clinical Stats of Patients with Bipolar Disorder. Bipolar Disorders, 2010
Editors, Religious and Spiritual Issues in Psychiatric Diagnosis: A Research Agenda for DSM-V. American Psychiatric Association Press, 2011.

Religion often promotes irrational, magical, and harmful thinking. It has been frequently observed, experienced, and reported in the media that religion can undermine the pursuit of science. By opposing scientific facts, religious campaigns significantly impact the daily lives of ordinary people. Religious policies that disregard proven scientific evidence can harm people's health and happiness. Today, religious doctrines and teachings influence public policies on medical treatments, homosexuality, abortion, contraception, and other issues, which often result in chaos and harm to people's health and well-being.

However, modern scientific discoveries and technological advancements are helping people become more conscious, logical, and rational. For many in our time, religious views on the biological, psychological, and spiritual aspects of human life are seen as untenable. People are no longer unconscious followers of maladaptive drives within themselves. They distance themselves from the narrow worldviews of religion and the limits these impose on the understanding of innate spiritual human nature.

Furthermore, in today's world, people's understanding of the ontological extends beyond the boundaries of religion and naive idealism. Evidence from life shows that there is an epistemic shift and deeper cultural sensitivities. People are capable of overriding the usual instinct for tribalism through deliberate and purposeful intention. More individuals recognize and understand that religious and spiritual phenomena are distinct and are discovering the spiritual as something greater than the narrow confines of religion.

In our times, the "spiritual" is more sought after when there are no perceived trappings of an organized religion's doctrines, rituals, traditions, and rules. This mainly results from a mindset influenced by the values of secularism and scientific rationalism. More people are willing to admit that religion's goal is often to guide a social group toward a certain way of thinking, feeling, and behaving. Many in our times believe religion is no longer relevant to human life as it is experienced and needs to be lived in the postmodern world.

People's disinterest in religion hasn't diminished their need for spiritual health. There is a clear desperation to improve spiritual well-being. More individuals are open to accepting the science behind spiritual health and acknowledge its benefits for overall health and quality of life. They recognize the importance of spiritual human nature and its role in daily life. However, a consequence of this trend is the increase in the proliferation of "spiritualism systems" in societies worldwide.

Traditionally, the term "spiritual" was used to describe a deeply religious person. But today, it also includes a completely secular person. Ordinary people often equate spirituality, spiritual life, and spiritualism with spiritual health. Sellers of spiritual ideologies and entrepreneurs involved in the "spiritual marketplace" are capitalizing on people's desire to improve their spiritual well-being. The "spiritual marketplace" is rapidly growing in modern society. The "spiritualism" of cults, "prosperity religions," and "spiritual products" offer shallow ideas of spiritual health.

In today's "spiritual marketplace,' the wide array of cult groups, prosperity religions, spiritual counseling and healing offices and parlors, yoga and retreat centers, and similar services create an illusion of promoting spiritual health. Critics warn that the "spiritual marketplace" adulterates ancient health philosophies and dilutes their true practices, uses questionable interpretations of religious scriptures and doctrines, and misapplies modern health sciences. Health experts criticize 'spiritualism' as an ego-soothing drug rather than an ego-dissolving drug. They argue it does little to foster self-growth or to satisfy the never-ending desires driven by consumerism. Spiritualism should be viewed as just another consumer product.

Health sciences approach spiritual health without relying on the paranormal, ethereal, or otherworldly visions often used for self-indulgence or ego gratification. Fundamental to developing spiritual health are processes like "renewing," "becoming," "wholeness," and "wholesomeness." It involves tuning into mental processes to understand one's inner-core reality as it relates to selfhood. It is about anchoring oneself in the true self through self-integration. The focus is on cultivating a wholesome personhood and a holistic life. Spiritualism, like religion, can distract people from the inner mental processes, the inner-core reality, and staying true to the real self.

For thousands of years, religion shaped perceptions of human nature that emphasized the spiritual side of life. It served as a force encouraging spiritual well-being among everyday people. Historical circumstances allowed religion to control the spiritual aspect of human existence. However, this is no longer true in our postmodern world for many straightforward reasons. We are now more rational, logical, pragmatic, and skeptical of anything related to health that isn't supported by scientific evidence. It is crucial for us today to differentiate between religious and spiritual experiences to recognize how a misnomer can diminish the importance of intentionally nurturing spiritual health in our lives.

Modern health sciences show that spiritual health is essential for achieving holistic human health. The documented evidence reveals that the "spiritual" aspect is interconnected with the physical, mental, and social parts of health. Health scientists emphasize that people's spiritual health leads to better affective and cognitive skills, as well as more stable psychological and emotional well-being. Researchers also present empirical evidence demonstrating that spiritual health helps reduce stress, anxiety, negative thoughts, feelings, and behaviors.[23] Most importantly, there is growing recognition that spiritual health is not only crucial in patient treatment but also vital for the well-being of healthy individuals.

To sum up:

---

[23] Gundersen L, Faith and Healing. Ann Intern Med Jan 2000 PubMed
Puchalski C, The Role of Spirituality in Healthcare. Baylor University Medical Center Proceedings (vol 14) October 2001 (PubMed)

More than what is known in the "religious way of life," people who cultivate spiritual health actively self-evolve. They stay attentive to life processes to support personal growth. Utopias of future life do not overshadow life as it unfolds in the present. The true self is the guiding principle in life. They develop the ability to self-regulate and self-direct.

When the focus is on nurturing spiritual well-being, people develop a sense of identity that's unique to their own experience, rather than one that's molded to fit a specific religious lifestyle. This deeper self-awareness and understanding of oneself allows for self-integration and personal growth without being held back by a rigid sense of self that's tied to a particular religion. As consciousness evolves, it helps create a self-identity that's more accepting and offers therapeutic benefits.

The goals and focus of developing spiritual health differ from those of a religious lifestyle. Religion often imposes "exclusivity blinders," leading to intolerance of differences and distancing those who do not share the same beliefs, values, and way of life. Many times, religion causes its followers to be hostile toward those who are not "believers."

The spiritual health of each person is connected to the health of humanity and the planet, just as it is connected to the individual's well-being. Evidence from life shows that people who develop spiritual health significantly contribute to creating a better society, a healthier humanity, and a healthier planet. Religion, as we experience it today, cannot claim to build a healthier society or humanity.

In our world, selfish, unethical, and immoral behaviors indicate a serious spiritual health crisis in our times, not a lack of religion. Religion is everywhere, like fast-food chains and restaurants. It's clear that religion has become a profitable business in our society. However, we belong to a corrupted humanity and navigate life within a depraved existence. Researchers in health sciences show that when people develop spiritual health, they tend to improve their ethical thinking and behaviors and foster healthy relationships.

The warnings and alarms from scientists and experts about global calamities highlight that humanity's well-being, and even that of the planet, depends on everyone's spiritual health, not any specific religion. Unfortunately, today's global culture tends to diminish the spiritual aspect of health in people.

Today's global culture blurs the line between virtue and vice to satisfy the hunger of the heart. It is an unfortunate tragedy that the spiritual health needed to heal and renew the human spirit is replaced with ego-soothing pursuits found in consumerist spiritualism and rigid religion. The true importance and urgency of spiritual health are diminished in the postmodern world.

Experts believe that if more people improve their spiritual health, it will lead to a wide range of positive benefits for the world, offering hopeful outcomes for humanity, the environment, and the planet.[24] The environmental challenges and issues in our world highlight the urgent need to restore the soul in human life. This results from developing spiritual health and does not happen simply through agreement with theological ideals or even the "religious way of life."

---

[24] Paloutzian RF and Park CL, Handbook of the Psychology of Religion and Spirituality. The Guilford Press, 2005

WHAT IS SPIRITUAL HEALTH

Today, we understand that human health is not confined to the physical body. It involves emotional, psychological, intellectual, spiritual, and social aspects, as well as society, humanity, the environment, and the planet. In health literature, the core dimensions of health are physical, mental, social, and spiritual, but many health experts also recognize the intellectual, psychological, emotional, moral, occupational, financial, and ecological dimensions.

Optimal human health is deeply holistic. Holistic health involves the integration of all aspects of well-being. It considers the development of complete personhood and a holistic lifestyle. Holistic health emphasizes that every part of a person's life is connected and influences their health. It is essential for a higher quality of life and forms the foundation of the "good life."

Since the beginning of the concept of health, the "spiritual" has always been seen as essential to good health and the way to develop holistic health. Throughout history, engaging the spiritual aspect of human nature has been vital in healthcare, treatment, and healing. There is ample evidence of this from many ancient cultures.

In ancient Greece, health involved the close connection of body and soul. Good health depended on a strong spiritual foundation. In his writings, Hippocrates stated that the vital force in nature—pneuma (spirit)—is what heals. The Greek words for 'cure,' which means "to repair a fractured soul," and 'nurse,' "to nurture the spirit," also point to this. In ancient Egypt, improving health involved warding off "bad spirits" that were controlling the body. Healing sanctuaries found in the ruins of ancient temples were used for rituals to cleanse possessed spirits. In ancient India, treatment and healing also focused on expelling "bad spirits." The Vedas, which document the ancient history of health practices in India, reveal healing involving spiritual elements. The Hindu concept of "aham brahmasi" suggests that spiritual human nature is essential to holistic personhood and health. In ancient Chinese health literature, the Huangdi Neijing, the cosmic theory of yin-yang dominated their system of medicine. This theory relates to earth and heaven elements—material and spiritual—for healing.

After the fall of the ancient civilizations, health knowledge did not progress until the seventeenth or eighteenth centuries. The conversion of Emperor Constantine to Christianity led to Christianity's dominance on the world stage. The Christian worldview introduced a theology-based understanding of human life and significantly influenced the development of ideas about health. This radically reshaped new perspectives on health.

According to the religious worldview of this period, health and healing were solely based on otherworldly influences. During medieval times, one cannot overstate the importance of the religious worldview in shaping human life. Health treatment became a matter of religious faith, involving rituals and prayers. The influence of religion was so strong that no one ever challenged religious perspectives on issues affecting human life, including health.

Religion encouraged an obsession with saving the soul for eternal life. The explanations and treatments of diseases were filled with superstitions. Church teachings emphasized that suffering and death were punishments from God. The doctrine of Original Sin led to negative views of human nature and earthly life. It created a divide between the body and soul, shifting focus away from health and healing since ancient times.

During the Renaissance, many critical thinkers expressed worldviews that contradicted religious beliefs. However, there was still no tradition of scientific medicine. The dogmatic view of human nature continued to limit the concept of health among ordinary people. In the West, health knowledge mainly depended on surviving Greek and Roman texts, which were preserved, although religious worldviews held greater sway. In the East, it was shaped by religious beliefs mixed with basic medicinal science. Healthcare and treatment consisted of a blend of ancient ideas and religious influences.

There were important discoveries and inventions during the Enlightenment Age. It led to a surge of ideas that freed people from narrow-minded views of religion and its superstitions. The new bold ideas aimed to improve human life and better understand health issues. The changing situation in healthcare meant that religion was no longer the blind man describing the elephant. The patient, not the provider, became the focus of the health world. This shift resulted in significantly better approaches to healthcare and treatment, leading to more favorable health outcomes.

Modern science and technology shifted the dominance of the religious worldview of human life. Scientific rationalism and discoveries significantly transformed people's thinking. There was a fact-based, more pragmatic, and existential approach to issues related to human life. New scientific discoveries about natural laws made the natural world less mysterious and less mythical concerning health. This led to the scientific, evidence-based understanding of health matters.

The increasingly rational perspective on human life and the universe led to a 'new mind' regarding the natural world, human nature, and health. It helped people detach from the influence of religion, especially concerning health issues. There was greater objectivity in understanding topics related to human health.

Pragmatism and scientific rationalism led to the growth of critical thinking and secular values. Doubts and suspicions increased among people regarding religious opinions and worldviews on everyday health issues. They acknowledged that religious views could have adverse effects on health matters. The terms "spiritual" and "religious" started to be recognized as different.

In modern health sciences, the harmony between the body, mind, and spirit is considered essential for improving health and achieving optimal health. Scientists and researchers show that the interactions among the human mind, body, and spirit are fundamental to healthcare and treatment. They confirm that these processes are positively influenced when people nurture spiritual health. Research evidence indicates that spiritual health plays a key role in enhancing all aspects of health.

In the post-modern world, there is more focus on spiritual health than ever before. Health sciences show that spiritual health is essential for good physical, mental, and social well-being. Human sciences emphasize that spiritual health plays a decisive role in creating a healthier humanity and planet. In the scientific community, spiritual health is not only seen as necessary for personal health but also for the health of society, humanity, and the planet.

Nowadays, attention to spiritual health is clearly shown in healthcare and health services. Health professionals now talk about the "spiritual" with patients and promote routines, lifestyles, and practices to enhance spiritual health. More support systems are available in schools, companies, workplaces, businesses, governments, and almost everywhere to foster spiritual well-being. Public discussions about the importance of spiritual health are increasing. There is no shortage of services and opportunities that widely support the spiritual aspect of human life.

Furthermore, more research is being conducted on the spiritual component of health than ever before. More researchers are exploring the connection between the spiritual component of health and other aspects of health. The extensive research to date provides strong evidence that spiritual health positively influences all aspects of health.

So, what is spiritual health? Defining spiritual health is both straightforward and complex. A simple explanation is that it relates to the non-physical aspects of life. It concerns matters of metaphysical reality in human existence. It involves the spiritual dimension of human nature in the pursuit of a meaningful life. It is connected to transcendental realities, such as the "higher self," soulful living, and higher ideals and purposes. It pertains to the innate human potential to enhance the quality of life, fostering a holistic human being and a healthier humanity.

Although spiritual health has not been comprehensively defined in health literature, it is generally seen as the non-physical part of human nature that influences a person's health, well-being, and happiness, as well as the health and welfare of society and humanity. Spiritual health is explained as evolving in human consciousness, self-growth, becoming a holistic person, and living holistically. Health experts measure aspects like self-transcendence and other-centeredness to make the idea of spiritual health more concrete.

Health sciences emphasize that the spiritual component of human nature is essential to human health, development, maturity, and overall existence. The innate spiritual aspect of human nature supports the metaphysical. The metaphysical is fundamental to what defines true humanity. Spiritual health is seen as stemming from harnessing the innate potential found within the metaphysical human nature.

In health literature, researchers view spiritual health as a multi-dimensional experience. It is described as the harmonious connection one feels within oneself (personal dimension), with others (social dimension), with nature (environmental dimension), and with the ultimate reality (transcendental dimension).[25] All of this highlights the metaphysical aspect of human nature.

In modern times, researchers and scientists believe that spiritual health is a fundamental human phenomenon. Importantly, they reveal that the

---

[25] Ganbhari R and Mohammedimehr, Identification of Dimensions and Indicators of Spiritual Health: A Qulalitative Study. Journal of Education and Health Promotion, December 2020 Dhar N, Chaturvedi SK, Nandan D. Spiritual Health Scale 2011: Defining and Measuring 4th Dimension of Health, 2011.

underlying basis of spiritual human nature is the unique neurobiology of humans, which forms the foundation upon which we build spiritual health. The neurobiological processes in humans support our ability to enhance human consciousness, which can lead to non-ordinary human experiences (exceptional spiritual experiences) and/or transcendental experiences. These are experiences that actively demonstrate the metaphysical aspects of human nature, and any ordinary person is capable of having them.

Ordinary people experience spiritual health as the flow of a "renewal energy" guiding a course of life that brings positive benefits to personal well-being, health, and relationships. As a way to improve health, they see this "renewal energy" supporting the body's natural balance, or homeostasis. They find that the flow of "renewal energy" helps create the mental stability needed every day. They develop a shift toward an other-centered life orientation and are filled with human virtues like empathy, compassion, and altruism.

In literature, experts compare this flow of "renewal energy" to a "silent life force" that positively enhances personal health, shapes human society, and benefits the health of both humanity and the planet. Health specialists view spiritual health as an inherent healing energy responsible for "renewing" life. It is the natural salutogenic potential within humans to promote health and reduce disease. Researchers are discovering that this "renewal energy" results from neurobiological processes. They are providing evidence of a neurological site where spiritual health originates.

Today, neuroscience shows that the phenomenon of spiritual health is an objectifiable, measurable, and verifiable part of human health. Neuroscientists argue that an individual's spiritual health is influenced through "spiritual experiences,' regardless of whether they are religious. Researchers examine spiritual health in relation to the evolution of human consciousness and self-development. In health literature, experts assert that the evolution of human consciousness is crucial for self-development and positively impacts all areas of human life. They highlight spiritual health as the process of renewing and reinvigorating individuals.

The primary need for developing spiritual health is the growth of human consciousness and self-improvement. Growing spiritual health aims to achieve the "wholeness" of self through lifelong self-evolution. Both human psychology and consciousness play roles in this process. While the psychological traits rooted in genetics are important, it is the evolving human consciousness that serves as the pathway to self-evolution.

To be the "whole" human person one can be, it is necessary to actively engage in self-evolution. Just like a computer that constantly updates its software to a better version, self-evolution aims at the best version of the human being. It is the only way to access our untapped potential, achieve fulfillment in life, and make a difference in the world. Although self-evolution is essential for improving personal health and happiness, it also positively impacts society and humanity as a whole.

Everyone experiences a sense of self about who they are, how they have been in the past, and how they want to be in the future. They consider what they have done and what they want to do, as well as where they want to go in life and be remembered long after they are gone. This sense of self is acceptable and therapeutic to the extent that it contributes to their well-being and health. However, it may or may not effectively support the goals of good health and the "good life' they pursue. Human personhood is a dynamic process aimed at exponential holistic growth. It becomes degraded when people are stuck in their ways, and their selfhood remains static.

When we know where we want to go in life and want to be remembered long after we are gone, we commit to self-evolution and human growth and maturity. Self-evolution is a lifelong process dependent on the level of one's human consciousness. Daily self-awareness and self-understanding that support self-evolution revolve around the level of the individual's human consciousness. A more effective and fulfilled human life involves evolving in human consciousness to achieve the highest form of one's human personhood.

Essentially, the cultivation of spiritual health aims to reach the high levels of human consciousness to promote self-evolution. Human consciousness is a fundamental part of human nature. Its development unfolds in real life as it happens, impacting our daily life, health, and happiness. Cultivating spiritual health is the only way to unlock the dormant potential of our natural spiritual human nature in everyday life.

Experts in human consciousness distinguish between ordinary and non-ordinary consciousness.[26] Ordinary consciousness is usually static in a person and does not change. It depends on social, cultural, and environmental influences. It limits our thinking, perceptions, and viewpoints, which shape how we live. It also blocks the full development of the human being by undermining the potential of spiritual human nature.

In contrast, non-ordinary consciousness differs from the typical everyday "waking" consciousness, featuring unique experiences that are more easily accessible to the working mind. It represents an altered state of awareness with a deeper perception of reality. This state develops the intuitive mind, which embodies the powers of the metaphysical human nature. Often, non-ordinary consciousness leads to altered perceptions of time and space, profound insights, increased creativity, a sense of interconnectedness, or deep introspection. That's why some refer to it as "unifying consciousness" when describing the experience of non-ordinary consciousness.

Human consciousness cannot be fully understood or experienced outside the natural order. The human brain grants us consciousness, which is embedded in its structure. It relies on the medial prefrontal cortex, a unique feature not found in other living beings.

Neuroscience shows that the brain can be made to function in ways

---

[26] Robert B., What is Self: A Study of the Spiritual Journey in Terms of Consciousness. Sentient Publications (2005)
Sayadamnsour A, The Relationship Between the Brain and Religion. Journal of Neurology (Vol 13) 2014

that help evolve human consciousness. Researchers in neuroscience have identified changes in brain mechanisms and measured shifts in consciousness levels during religious and spiritual practices. Neuroscientists demonstrate that evolving human consciousness produces positive changes in brain functions, enhancing the human mind.[27]

The evolution of human consciousness has many implications for human life. The individual developing in human consciousness gains all-encompassing life perspectives and worldviews. The evolving human consciousness creates more effective mental and emotional maps to guide the way we live. People advancing in human consciousness are guided by higher-order thinking, which positively affects daily values, priorities, drives, and behaviors. This, in turn, benefits social and environmental aspects of human life, as well as personal well-being and happiness.

In practical terms, spiritual health is about living one's most free and fullest life. To do so is to live from the inside out. Spiritual health builds on the energizing potential of the inner-core reality and the true self to create soulfulness in life. People who experience the benefits of spiritual health point to the content of the inner-core reality, which can positively or negatively influence every aspect of one's life.

The potential of an "unseen reality" within each person — the inner-core reality — is always brought to life and made real in daily experience, whether intentionally or not. Since ancient times, people have paid attention to their inner core to grow, improve, and mature as individuals. Today, health providers often explore issues of the inner core to promote healing and support individuals in improving their health. In health science literature, growing spiritual health consistently involves focusing on one's inner-core reality and

---

[27] Ashbrook JB, Albright CR, The Humanizing Brain: Where Religion and Neuroscience Meet. Pilgrim Press 1997
Newberg AB, Neuroscience and Religion: Neureotheology, Encyclopedia of Religion. (2nd ed) Macmillian 2005

the true self.

The inner core defines a person's essence and motivations for a consistent way of life. It shapes the inner disposition for values, attitudes, perceptions, and preferences, as well as negative tendencies and behaviors. Life habits, relationship styles, and every expression of a person's selfhood mirror the inner-core reality.

Health science literature sees the inner-core reality as essential for developing good health. Cross-cultural studies suggest the inner-core reality as a source of an individual's personal power. Modern psychology states that the inner-core reality has the potential to foster positive aspirations, behaviors, and relationships.

The inner-core reality is a strong central connection that links all aspects of health. It has the power to bring about both positive and negative effects on every component of health. The inner-core reality shapes or empties out a person's health. It can be a force that either enriches life or destroys it. The inner core has the potential to enhance psycho-emotional stability and foster a holistic person.

The inner-core reality is fundamental to personhood, whether it's a "whole" or "fragmented" one. The sense of self is deeply rooted in the individual's inner core. It shapes the self that may be complete or in pieces. At all times, it can draw attention to or distract from the process of self-evolution and personal growth. It can inspire personal change and growth to stay true to one's real self. Through the inner core, a person can reveal what is sublime or shocking in human nature.

In every living moment, the core reality is a potential for both a "spiritual core" and a "malevolent core." Either can influence who a person becomes at any given time. The "spiritual core" expresses the metaphysical essence within human reality, serving as the path to the true self. The "malevolent core" dehumanizes individuals by undermining the metaphysical essence of human nature and aligning with the pseudo-self.

The cognitive access to one's true self primarily occurs by tuning into the mind's processes. These processes are heavily influenced by the individual's inner-core reality. Today, health sciences provide empirical evidence suggesting that experiencing a meaningful life is linked to having cognitive access to one's true self. Modern psychology emphasizes that the true self resides deep within the psyche. It highlights that psychological factors, unique to each person, can either facilitate or hinder access to the true self.

Health researchers and experts have observed that individuals with high levels of spiritual health tend to prioritize the "real self" over the "ideal self," "actual self," and the "pseudo-self." Since ancient times, philosophers have discussed the real self as influencing personality and health differently than the pseudo-self. The inner-core reality acts as a bridge between the "ideal self" or "actual self" and the "real self," helping to distance oneself from the "pseudo-self." This process occurs as people develop spiritual health. They remain attuned to their mental processes, influenced by the inner-core reality, to engage in the "renewing" and "becoming" processes of self-evolution.

The "ideal self" and "actual self" – the person we normally show in daily life – do not always reflect the "real self." When we are unaware of our mental processes, the "real self" is not distinguished from the "actual self" or "pseudo self." Therefore, the "actual self" and "pseudo self," which others often see, might not always represent the "real self," which is the objective, fact-based person, the actual human reality of someone's selfhood.

The way a person approaches life may or may not originate from the "spiritual core" and the "real self." People may or may not utilize the resources of the "spiritual core" and the "real self" to cultivate strong health and happiness. These lesser-known resources are used to create fulfillment in human life and to enhance society's well-being. Few realize that when someone's life orientation is rooted in the real self, they are entirely free to live on their own terms.

The effort to stay true to the real self opens the way to discover the higher self. In health literature, the higher self is seen as the peak of human consciousness. Essentially, spiritual health entails adhering to a path guided by the inner core, the true self, and the higher self. The highest level of spiritual health is demonstrated when people reach their peak in human consciousness, experienced as the higher-order personhood or higher self. Essentially, the "whole" human being lives from the "higher self."

Ordinary people who nurture and maintain good spiritual health find a comfortable space within themselves for calm, peace, and harmony. They demonstrate stronger abilities to cope with and effectively handle the countless problems, struggles, and stressors of daily life. They are more aware of both internal and external factors and conditions that influence matters of health and human quality of life. They have a deeper understanding of the underlying elements that harm health and those that positively contribute to holistic well-being. They remain tuned to the complex workings of the human body to sustain homeostasis.

When people develop spiritual health, they focus more on the "inner world" than on externals. They strive for higher purposes and ideals in human life. They express life motivations aimed at "spiritual prosperity" in all areas of human existence. They demonstrate greater human sensitivity and awareness for connection within the web of life by emphasizing the principles of interdependence, human solidarity, and coexistence in everyday life. Psychosocial maturity in regular daily relationships benefits both oneself and others.

None of this can occur without the development of human consciousness. It is essential for advancing higher cognitive functions of the mind, like sense perceptions, intuition, and deeper insights. To unlock dormant "spiritual capacities" such as transcendence, connectivity, and ethicality, we depend on the higher cognitive abilities of the mind. The commitment to improving the quality of human life for everyone, the health of humanity, and caring for the planet requires the evolution of consciousness and self-evolution.

It happens when people nurture and sustain spiritual health.

NEUROSCIENCE OF SPIRITUAL HEALTH

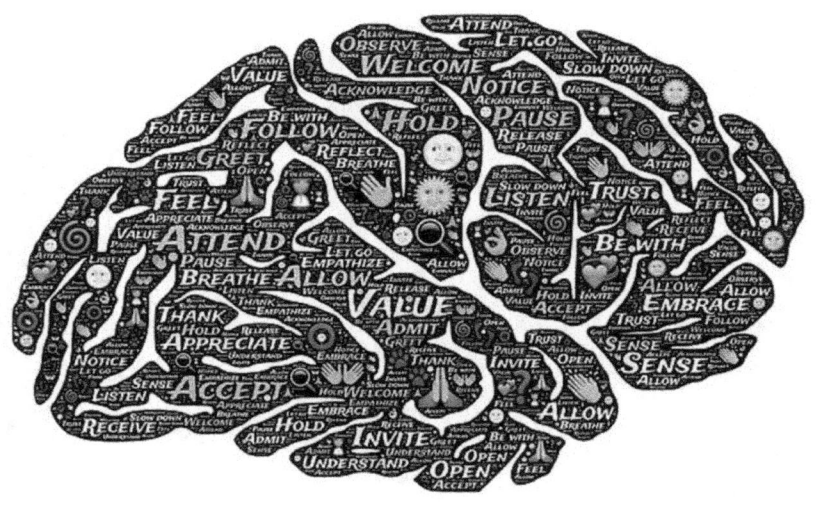

Neurobiological Foundations of Spiritual Health
Image from Creative Commons Zero

This image effectively illustrates the human brain during the multidimensional experiences of spiritual health. Thanks to discoveries in neuroscience, we now understand how spiritual health is cultivated and how this cultivation relates to brain regions, mechanisms, and functions in everyday life.

This chapter aims to help the reader understand how the complex "ordinary" human organism can become "extraordinary" through the potential of the inherent spiritual human nature. The terms and concepts of neuroscience are not everyday language. Scientific jargon can be confusing. I have tried to present the neuroscience of spiritual health in a way that is easy for the reader to grasp.

From the start, it is important to emphasize that the supremacy of human personhood is demonstrated by attaining the "spiritual capacities" of the "extraordinary" human organism. Human nature uniquely endows us with spiritual capacities, and anyone can develop these abilities if they are intentional and deliberate in doing so.

Neuroscience is an exciting and emerging health science that aims to understand the most complex organ in the body – the brain. It examines the brain's anatomy, function, and chemistry. Drawing from various fields of science – from molecular biology to the psychological study of the mind – neuroscience has, over the past several decades, investigated how the brain's functioning impacts health. It shows that many health issues are linked to the neurobiological processes occurring in the human brain.

Neuroscience explores questions about the nervous system related to health by studying how the brain works and how brain chemicals change. It proposes neurobiological processes to understand issues like the mind-body connection affecting health, the impact of stress, deviant behaviors, and more. Recently, neuroscience has also investigated cognitive and emotional abilities, transcendental experiences, innate human potentials, and non-ordinary experiences in human life, many of which are closely connected to spiritual health.

The research conducted so far in neuroscience has significantly enhanced our understanding of the neural functions underlying human nature and the human spirit in relation to holistic health. There are numerous benefits from neuroscience that help us improve health and the quality of our lives.

Researchers in neuroscience, genetics, and epidemiology agree that humans possess a spiritual nature. They have confirmed that the spiritual is innate to human nature and that spiritual capacities are exclusive to the human species. The research conducted so far highlights that innate spiritual human nature plays a central role in how we live the "human" life. It is essential for building a healthy society and humanity.

Several neuroscientists have researched how religious and spiritual practices affect the human brain.[28] All have identified a common pattern of neurological activity across different types of spiritual and religious experiences. The evidence shows that daily practices of "spiritual technologies" help people stay grounded, strong, and resilient, which is only partially achieved through the "religious way of life."

Neuroscience research studies validate the spiritual nature of humans as a way to improve the brain's mechanisms and functions. Neuroscience shows that the spiritual aspect of human nature has the potential to rewire the brain. Therefore, through enhanced brain mechanisms and beneficial changes in brain chemistry, the spiritual side of humans can lead to positive developments in the mind, favorably impacting all aspects of human life and existence. This evidence causes neuroscientists to affirm that there is a spiritual component to health.

Those who study the neurobiological basis of spiritual health recognize that these phenomena have the potential to positively influence human life and existence in ways different from without them.

Though still in its early stages, the neuroscience of religious and spiritual phenomena has made significant progress since some of the initial

---

[28] Dietrich A. <u>Functional Neuroanatomy of Altered States of Consciousness: The Transient Hypofrontality Hypothesis</u>. Conscious Cogn. 12(2) (2003)
Mueller PS, Plevak DJ, Rummans TA. <u>Religious Involvement, Spirituality, and Medicine: Implications for Clinical Practice.</u> Mayo Clin Proc. 76(12) 2001
Kjaer TW, Bertelsen C, et.al. <u>Increased Dopamine Tone Suring Meditation-induced Change of Consciousness.</u> Brain Res Cogn Brain 13(2) 2002.

studies conducted about four decades ago. Today, neuroscience helps us better understand the neurobiological processes behind spiritual experiences in healing and health. The neuroscience of spiritual health introduces a bold new paradigm for health, healing, and resilience.

What neuroscientists have identified occurring during religious and spiritual practices is called "non-ordinary human experiences" (I am calling them "spiritual experiences"). The brain mechanisms and chemistry are found to improve and change during such experiences. Some neuroscientists refer to the observable changes as the "awakened brain." They argue that there is a "spiritual brain" system affected by spiritual human nature and consider it essential for enhancing spiritual health. There is little doubt within the scientific community that improved human brain processes are a result of human evolution and are fundamental to spiritual human nature.

As the study of spiritual health continues to expand, more discoveries are being made about how human biology, particularly neurobiology, is vital to developing spiritual well-being. Neuroscience reveals that the cognitive and emotional processes of the human mind that support spiritual health are influenced by specific brain regions, neural mechanisms, and brain chemistry.

Researchers have shown that "non-ordinary human experiences" – spiritual experiences – during religious and spiritual practices enhance neurobiological processes, leading to atypical cognitive and emotional abilities that have a "transformational effect" on human personhood and promote spiritual health. They emphasize that "non-ordinary human experiences" during these practices rewire the brain and alter brain chemistry to positively influence the thinking, feeling, and behavioral signs of the spiritual health phenomena a person experiences.

Neuroscientists assert that the "spiritual brain" creates a "spiritual condition" (which I refer to as "spiritual health"). The experience of this "spiritual condition" – spiritual health – significantly enhances cognitive functions, psycho-emotional stability, and an objective sense of self, leading to a more meaningful life. They believe the "spiritual brain" can clarify the human mind, reduce stress and negative emotions, and serve as a resource for overall health improvement.

Neuroscience is showing that spiritual health gives people stronger grit, optimism, and resilience. It also enhances the human brain's ability to protect against addiction, trauma, and depression—ultimately leading to a more joyful and fulfilling life. Researchers discovered that the "spiritual brain" provides psycho-emotional clarity and fosters a deeper sense of equanimity, aiding in self-acceptance and self-esteem. This enables individuals to thrive better in personal and social spheres, contributing to a healthier humanity. People experience objectivity, self-coherence, and a sense of wholeness in personhood, creating harmony and peace within themselves and with others.[29]

Researchers in neuroscience have also discovered that increased heart rate variability, lower blood pressure, stress hormones (such as cortisol), and improved immune system function are indirect effects of growing spiritual health. Arguably, these effects can lead to a reduced risk of heart disease, stroke, cancer, infections, and other chronic conditions.[30]

Furthermore, they highlight the benefits of the "spiritual brain" on human psychology and behavior. They discovered that through religious and spiritual practices, the "spiritual brain" also helps reduce symptoms of mental illnesses and protects against addictive behaviors. Today, neuroscience provides substantial insights into many broader aspects of people's overall health related to high levels of spiritual well-being.

To help clarify the neurobiological mechanisms linked to spiritual health, neuroscientists gather information using neurobiological measures such as electroencephalographic activity, cerebral blood flow, cerebral metabolism,

---

[29] Yaden DB, Haid J, and Newberg A. The Varieties of Self-Transcendent Experience. The Jounral of Positive Psychology; June, 2017
[30] Hye-Geum K, et. al. Stress and Heart Rate Variability: A Meta-analysis and Review of the Literature. Psychiatry Investig., March 2018

and neurotransmitter activity. They also assess physiological parameters like blood pressure, body temperature, heart rate, and galvanic skin responses. Additional factors such as immunological tests, hormonal levels, and autonomic activity offer a comprehensive analysis of the experiential effects of the "spiritual experience," leading to the "spiritual condition" of individuals.

What neuroscience has shown is that the human brain and nervous system make the human species neurologically unique and distinguishable from the rest of nature. Humans are uniquely endowed with a neurobiological potential for "spiritual experiences," which underpins innate "spiritual capacities." Neuroscience indicates that spiritual health is fundamentally both a product of nature and nurture. While spiritual health depends on the functions of the brain and nervous system, it is cultivated when culture and environment tap into the neurobiological potential for it to develop.

Before delving into the specifics of the neuroscience of spiritual health, it is important to gain some familiarity with the brain and nervous system. Most people know the brain is divided into two hemispheres, commonly called the right brain and the left brain. They are connected by the corpus callosum, which allows communication between them. The cortex is the outer layer of the brain that includes the frontal, parietal, temporal, and occipital lobes, and it is responsible for high-level functions like decision-making. It plays a key role in our personality and daily functioning. Beneath the cortex is the subcortex, which includes the basal ganglia, hypothalamus, thalamus, and cerebellum. These structures are responsible for primitive brain functions such as emotions and impulses.

The brain is the control center of the nervous system. It processes information within the nervous system. The nervous system is the part of the body that enables organisms to interact with their environments. It is divided into the central nervous system and the peripheral nervous system. The central nervous system consists of the brain and spinal cord, while the peripheral nervous system comprises nerves that extend from the spinal cord to all parts of the body.

The peripheral nervous system is part of the autonomic nervous system that transmits information between the brain and the body, including unconscious functions like heart rate and breathing. The autonomic nervous system divides into the sympathetic and parasympathetic nervous systems. The sympathetic branch is responsible for the "fight or flight" response, while the parasympathetic branch manages the "relaxation response."

Brain cells, called neurons, communicate through neurotransmitters. These neurotransmitters send messages between brain cells via neuro-electrical signals, also known as neurochemical processes. They are made up of various building blocks like amino acids, peptides, and monoamines. Examples include glutamate, serotonin, and dopamine. Neuroscientists have discovered that the "spiritual experience" from religious and spiritual practices positively influences the activity of neurotransmitters at synapses.

Neurochemistry is now helping us understand the effects of the "spiritual experience" – specifically, how neurotransmitters shape the "spiritual brain" through changes in brain chemistry. More explanation of how religious and spiritual practices affect brain chemistry will be provided later in the chapter.

Neuroscience has more specifically identified the neurobiological processes involving the parietal lobes, frontal lobes, thalamus, and the nervous system as related to spiritual human nature. These neurobiological processes provide evidence that human nature is endowed with "spiritual capacities" and play essential roles in developing spiritual health. This is due to the neurocircuits and neurochemicals within the human brain and nervous system functioning through the interactive processes of internal and external conditions. This interactive process is explained further below.

Researchers agree that neurobiological changes occur in the brain during various religious and spiritual phenomena. They point out that these changes are consistently associated with the occurrence of "spiritual experiences" during religious and spiritual practices. The frontal lobes, parietal lobes, thalamus, and limbic system in the brain are often involved in these neurobiological changes during "spiritual experiences."

The neurochemical and hormonal interactions among various parts of the central nervous system influence the processes of "spiritual experiences" and the "spiritual condition." The brain communicates internally among the cortex, hypothalamus, hippocampus, amygdala, and limbic system to produce "spiritual experiences" that lead to the "spiritual condition."

Neuroscience shows that the effect of "spiritual experiences" on the "spiritual condition" is connected to neurobiological processes that support better functioning of the human mind. These processes enhance cognition, emotions, and consciousness, which positively influence the transformation of human personhood, evident in overall health and holistic development.

The processes of "spiritual experiences" are governed by the prefrontal cortex, along with the temporal lobes and the hypothalamus, which manages hormonal regulation. The hippocampus links the individual to the external world, the amygdala controls how the individual responds to it, and most notably, the limbic system adds the emotional component to the "spiritual condition."

Neuroscience identifies the parietal cortex, specifically the left inferior parietal lobule, as the neurobiological location of the "spiritual brain" associated with developing spiritual health. This part of the brain is called the "neurobiological home" of spiritual health in neuroscience. It becomes active during "spiritual experiences," whether or not the trigger is religious.

Scientists have demonstrated that the left inferior parietal lobule plays a key role in perceptual processing that forms mental representations of the self, others, and the world. It contributes to the "spiritual condition" in humans during "spiritual experiences." The "spiritual condition" enhances perception and acts as a buffer against the adverse effects of stress on health. Marc Potenza, a Yale University scientist and psychiatry professor, described the "spiritual condition" (spiritual health) as a strong state that significantly influences the entire human person, helping them live more effectively.[31]

Neuroscientists demonstrate that the neural activity associated with the "spiritual experience" during spiritual and religious practices positively impacts the psychological, affective, and cognitive brain structures.[32] The research reveals that during the "spiritual experience" event, the experiential facet strengthens the "spiritual condition" of the human person, benefiting how people live in the world and helping improve society's health.

Andrew Newberg, a neuroscientist and pioneer of "neurotheology," focused on the connection between the brain and the experiential aspect of "spiritual experiences." Newberg examined brain scans of individuals who report high levels of "spiritual condition" and discovered that religious and spiritual practices can modify the thalamus. The thalamus, which is involved in sensory processing and shaping perceptions of reality by linking various cortical areas, is affected by these practices. This altered state of the thalamus, facilitated by spiritual practices, enhances cognitive processing and emotional responses.[33]

Researchers observed that the "spiritual condition" of a person is a state characterized by neural relaxation.[34] They claim the experiential aspect of "spiritual experiences" leads to reduced activity in the left inferior parietal lobule. They also found that the brain's medial thalamus and caudate, which are involved in sensory and emotional processing, become less responsive during the "spiritual condition" compared to when responding to stressful stimuli. Additionally, the parietal cortex becomes active whenever individuals experience a sense of connection within themselves and their surroundings.

Neuroscience has identified the deep roots of spiritual health in a part

---

[31] Potenza, MN, Perspective: Behavioral Addictions Matters. Nature, June 2015
[32] Fineberg NA, Chamberlain SR, Ponteza MN, et.al. New Developments in Human Neurocognition: Clinical, Genetic and Brain Imaging Correlates of Impulsivity and Compulsivity. Cambridge University Press, February 2014
[33] Newberg AB, The Neuroscientific Study of Spiritual Practices. Front Psychol, 2014
[34] Newberg AB, How Enlightenment Changes Your Brain. Penguim House 2016

of the human brain called the periaqueductal gray (PAG). This brainstem region is involved in many functions, including fear conditioning, pain modulation, empathy, altruism, and unconditional love. These essential functions are central to our understanding of what it means to be human. They reveal the metaphysical essence of personhood and highlight the spiritual aspect of human nature, which is fundamental to human reality. These functions are grounded in neurobiological processes and are intricately woven into the neurofabric of human nature. Neuroscientists see the PAG as crucial for developing the "spiritual brain" and maintaining spiritual health. They also show that spiritual and religious practices positively influence the brain circuit involving the PAG.

Neurochemistry shows that the neurotransmitter serotonin influences parts of the brain involved in emotions and perceptions. Fourteen serotonin receptor subtypes have been identified in the human brain. Neuroscientists have discovered that serotonin affects the process of "spiritual experiences."[35] The neurons originate from the raphe nuclei in the brainstem and connect to major brain regions such as the hypothalamus, the limbic system, the striatum, and the neocortex. When people engage in spiritual practices like meditation, researchers found that the front part of the brain (the attention-orientation region) helps increase serotonin levels.

Of course, it is more complex than that. There are other chemicals and receptors involved in people's spiritual experiences. Researchers have discovered that the serotonin system is not the only brain neurotransmitter system connected to spiritual experiences. The dopamine system is also involved. Neuroscientists have shown that spiritual experiences activate the brain's reward circuits in the same way as love, sex, gambling, drugs, and music. The process of having spiritual experiences is known to increase dopamine levels, the feel-good neurotransmitter that helps stabilize mood.

Researchers identified dominant parasympathetic activity—the

---

[35] Kurup RK and Kurup AP, Hypothalamic Digoxin, Hemispheric Chemical Dominance, and Spirituality. International Journal of Neuroscience (Vol 113), 2009

relaxation response of the autonomic nervous system—during religious and spiritual practices.[36] There was a decrease in heart rate, blood pressure, respiratory rate, and oxygen metabolism. The hormonal changes linked to spiritual practices include cortisol, noradrenaline, endorphins, sex hormones, and growth hormone.

Neuroscience has shown that the human brain can reorganize itself structurally in response to various events. Neural networks focus on connectivity, association, and identification. Scientists have discovered that when neurons fire together, they wire together. This relates to the brain's ability to transform itself. Neuroplasticity is an almost miraculous capacity of the human brain to reorganize itself to access higher, non-discriminating aspects of human potential. It highlights the plasticity of the human brain underlying the "spiritual experience" and "spiritual condition."[37]

Neuroscientists emphasize that many neural networks are subconscious or unconscious processes in the human mind. This is because humans are genetically programmed based on the principles of fear and survival. The survival instinct shapes the patterns of the mind. The experiential map of typical neural networks related to fear and survival reduces brain activity, making it difficult for a person to see alternative new routes.

Neuroplasticity involves relinquishing the fixed patterns or pathways in the neural network. It enables new patterns to develop. Andrew Weil – an internationally recognized expert on healthy lifestyles – maintains that, among other things, neuroplasticity means that positive mental and emotional states can be cultivated in much the same way that a person can learn to play golf, basketball, or master a musical instrument. He asserts that through repetition, such practices change both the activity and the physical aspects of specific brain

---

[36] Newberg AB, How Enlightenment Changes Your Brain. Penguim Random House, 2016
[37] Ashbrook JB, Albright CR, The Humanizing Brain: Where Religion and Neuroscience Meet. Pilgrim Press 1997
Newberg AB, Neuroscience and Religion: Neureotheology, Encyclopedia of Religion. (2nd ed) Macmillian 2005

areas.[38]

Andrew Newberg and Mark Walsman's study on neuroplasticity supports the idea that spiritual practices help people handle life's stressors with less negativity and greater self-regulation and compassion. In their own words, "When you intently and consistently focus on your spiritual values and goals, you increase the blood flow to your frontal lobes and anterior cingulate, which causes the activity in the emotional centers of the brain to decrease."[39]

In the book, How God Changes Your Brain, they highlight a wide range of Eastern and Western spiritual and religious practices that alter brain mechanisms and chemistry to boost people's health and improve the quality of human life. They stress that spiritual and religious practices strengthen specific neurological circuits and promote physiological balance, mental stability, social awareness, and compassion for others. The book is regarded as both an insightful work on neuroscience and a practical guide for readers to enhance their spiritual health.

Newberg asserts that religious and spiritual practices generating "spiritual experiences" benefit people in various psychological areas, enhance resilience, and support positive emotional processes such as acceptance of self and others, compassion, love, and altruism. The improvements in brain mechanisms and chemistry through "spiritual experiences" always positively impact all aspects of human health.

Neuroplasticity is about the fundamental healing ability of the human brain. The neuroplasticity of the human brain helps create the unified consciousness of the human mind, which is different from the dual consciousness that the human mind is often subject to. It frees the human mind from the fixed binary thinking system of ordinary default dual consciousness. This means that human consciousness allows people to move beyond

---

[38] Weil, A., & Chiasson, AM, Self-Healing with Energy Medicine. Sounds True 2009
[39] Newberg AB and Walsman, M.R. How God Changes Your Brain. Penguim Random House, 2009

predetermined reactions in life.

Neuroscience considers that the aspect of "attending awareness" in daily life is always critical to the change and transformation of predetermined neural networks. When we grow in spiritual health, the patterns of activity in the parietal cortex evolve the "attending awareness" of unifying consciousness. The evolved consciousness forges all-encompassing perspectives and the sense of "oneness," experienced as the well-balanced, well-integrated, whole person.

The human brain's functional connectivity is linked to the frequency of brainwaves. We can measure brainwaves with an electroencephalogram (EEG). Brainwaves largely influence human consciousness, self-awareness, and the feeling of interconnectedness in life. Researchers using EEG have shown how 'fragmented' or out-of-sync one's entire brain activity can often be. This fragmented activity leads to the fragmented mind we commonly experience while navigating life. Such fragmentation is often evident in conflicts among a person's thoughts, feelings, and behaviors.

On the other hand, people who have high levels of spiritual health show more 'harmonious' brain waves, which experts say indicate greater synchrony or connectivity within and across different neural areas. In short, when people develop their spiritual health, there are physiological effects in the brain and body, and the EEG offers a view into these changes.

Ordinary people who regularly engage in spiritual practices promote greater connection and neural synchronization. Neuroscientists have observed a symphony of brain cells—a higher level of synchronization—when individuals engage in spiritual practices. This neuronal synchronization improves the brain's 'harmony' or 'integrity,' helping the brain function more cohesively and incorporate broader perspectives in human life.

Neuroscience shows that increased neuronal synchronization in the brain helps people develop their natural spiritual abilities, such as transcendence, otherness, sense perception, insight, intuition, and practical wisdom. They become more effective in how they live and better manage all aspects of health. In practical terms, they foster values, attitudes, priorities, and broader perspectives, as well as improved judgment, to solve everyday problems creatively.

In conclusion, the effects of religious and spiritual practices have far-reaching impacts on the human person than are usually perceived or understood. The "spiritual" is not just a theoretical idea about human life but an inherent potential that influences human life. It is an intricate phenomenon that affects holistic health, which we may either experience or deny.

Research in neuroscience shows that improved brain function is vital for better health and quality of life. It highlights that brain mechanisms and chemistry play a role in developing spiritual health. Scientific evidence confirms that many time-tested spiritual principles and practices, like ethicality and meditation, are closely connected to changes in the brain and other parts of the body.

Today, we have a better understanding of the role of the "spiritual" component of human nature in our health and quality of life. We know that spiritual human nature has a neural basis and that spiritual health has neurological foundations. More people are willing to distinguish between spiritual and religious phenomena. More are seeking science-based practices to grow and improve spiritual health, recognizing that it is closely linked to holistic health.

Lastly, without prejudice, it must also be noted that some have interpreted neuroscience as offering new support for a materialist view of human nature. It is argued that neuroplasticity research signifies a significant shift in how the "spiritual" is viewed within reductionist materialist perspectives.

THE CHALLENGING TASK OF SPIRITUAL HEALTHCARE

Throughout life, health care is the only ongoing and consistent task we undertake. It is the only way to promote good health and prevent disease. Health care is like a never-ending journey, and the path to a "healthy me" can be challenging. It becomes even harder in a world driven by speed and the pursuit of pleasure. For most of us, unfortunately, the journey to a "healthy me" often begins only after a health crisis or a life-changing event.

We are generally indifferent or neglectful of health issues until we become ill. Additionally, we tend to focus only on the physical and mental aspects of health. We aren't equally committed to healthcare and treatment in other areas, such as spiritual, moral, and social health. We rarely concentrate on and invest little in our spiritual health. Few recognize spiritual health as having the potential to enhance overall health, well-being, and quality of life. Even fewer seek it out as a resource to improve the health of society, humanity, and the planet.

Often, during a sudden health crisis, people realize that there is more to life than just the physical, sensual, and perceptual experiences. In such moments, they instinctively connect with the spiritual dimension of life. This creates worldviews that allow them to engage with life through their innate spiritual human nature. The limits of the material human nature are acknowledged, along with how they influence healthcare. They learn to approach life with the potential of their spiritual human nature to achieve healing and recovery. For some, then, cultivating spiritual health becomes essential on the journey to a "healthy me."

When people map the journey of life with spiritual human nature, they develop values, priorities, and attitudes that enrich life and positively improve its quality. When they recognize that spiritual human nature underpins optimal health and happiness, it encourages them to consider matters often overlooked daily. This awareness helps them make the right choices and good decisions to stay on the path to a "healthy me." They emphasize growing spiritual health as a vital part of healthcare.

The only way to achieve good and complete health is by consistently staying in the "health lane." However, as with any long journey, it's inevitable to face distractions, monotony, drudgery, and fatigue Additionally, some people may face unique challenges and issues, such as mental and physical conditions or disabilities. The path to a "healthy me" doesn't avoid challenges and struggles. During these times, one doesn't change the direction but, like a skilled pilot, stays focused, thinks responsibly, and acts sensibly through life's ups and downs.

When committed to staying in the "health lane," there is always the realization that spiritual health plays a crucial role in overcoming hazards and harmful conditions on the way to the "healthy me." One explores realities that are greater than the sensual, fleeting, and transitional ones. We acknowledge that spiritual health grounds us during tough and challenging moments in the journey.

When spiritual health is emphasized, the motivation in daily life centers on self-growth and holistic living. A person's sense of meaning and purpose encompasses others, the environment, and the creation of a better world for everyone. Pursuing higher ideals, the common good, and principles that enhance life shape daily choices, decisions, and actions. Throughout the challenging landscape of human existence, everything that fosters spiritual health supports the journey toward a "healthy me."

When there is a focus on spiritual health, people tend to prefer lifestyles that support holistic health and holistic living. They emphasize preventive healthcare over curative healthcare. They set life goals aimed at higher ideals, purposes, and the common good. They connect holistic living to the "good life," life fulfillment, and human happiness.

Usually, we focus on the physical and mental parts of health. The importance of spiritual health is often overlooked. This is due to some factors specific to the modern world. One of these relates to the definition of health.

The official definition of health appears unclear about the spiritual aspect. In the words of the WHO definition, health is "a complete state of physical, mental, and social well-being, and not merely the absence of disease or sickness."[40] It seems to overlook the spiritual component of health.

The WHO defines health as the optimal functioning of a person, but the emphasis in this definition is solely on the physical, mental, social, and environmental determinants of health. It doesn't address the spiritual determinant of health. The definition may suggest that spiritual human nature and spiritual health are less relevant to the concept of health.

Critics argue that by excluding the spiritual component, the WHO definition fails to encompass the full range of health determinants. The lack of explicit mention of the "spiritual" in the definition dismisses the spiritual aspect of health. It hides the importance of spiritual health in healthcare, human life, and human existence.

Many argue that the official definition of health is the primary reason society neglects and ignores spiritual health. They believe that omitting the spiritual aspect from the official definition has led to policies and programs at

---

[40] WHO Constitution

local, national, and international levels overlooking people's spiritual health. Without emphasizing spiritual health, humans have become more vulnerable to spiritual problems, which can lead to moral decline and a worsening moral environment in the world.

Some argue that the WHO definition excludes the spiritual determinant of health because of the historical connection between the spiritual and religious. They say that the WHO did not intend for religion to be seen as a core part of health because people often think that religious and spiritual phenomena are the same.

For many millennia, the spiritual has been closely tied to religion. The clear distinction between spiritual and religious phenomena is a modern development. Modern scientific discoveries in health and medical sciences regularly demystify and demythologize what was once considered "spiritual" in religious phenomena.

Although the connection between spiritual and religious phenomena has been separated, the belief that they are the same remains deeply rooted in collective thinking. The confusion about what truly constitutes spirituality persists today. When facing life's challenges, ordinary people often turn to religion as their only known source of the "spiritual." They have not yet moved beyond the old ideas to see it differently.

When life gets tough, it becomes clear that the spiritual side of life takes priority, yet it often gets neglected otherwise. Many people's idea of spiritual strength is tied up with strict religious practices. Spiritual well-being is usually overlooked as a crucial part of overall health, human life, and existence. As a result, the spiritual aspect of health often receives insufficient attention in daily life.

For many centuries, religions have created a deep and false divide between science and the spiritual. The worldview of science was often rejected in the framework of religion. The "spiritual" was overshadowed by theological views, religious beliefs, and rituals. Religious dogma and rituals defined the "spiritual" not as something inherent to human nature but as otherworldly and celestial. The consequences of this divide are clear today, as people distance themselves from religion and show growing indifference toward spiritual health.

Another reason for neglecting spiritual health is the global culture that is unique to our times. In the postmodern world, the emphasis on individualism, materialism, consumerism, and hedonism effectively obscures the innate human awareness of the spiritual dimension of life. It suppresses the need to nurture spiritual health. The spiritual essence of human nature is diverted by the material pursuits of people's life goals.

Lifestyles, life priorities, and goals are shaped more by the material aspects of human nature than by the spiritual. The constant influence of technology and materialism today overwhelmingly shapes how we define being human. The pursuit of possessions and success, along with a hedonistic lifestyle, takes priority over what is truly essential for human life. What genuinely influences well-being and health is often overlooked in life pursuits. The dominance of material human nature guides our idea of the "good life" and determines how we seek human fulfillment.

Yet another reason, unique to the postmodern world, for neglecting spiritual health is the bureaucratic transformation of health systems. Modern treatment and care rely more on machines and less on the therapeutic skills of providers. Advances in modern technology have radically changed how we think about health. These technological advances in medicine have brought about significant changes in how people understand health care, treatment, and cures. The regular use of machines like MRI and X-ray scanners, along with wearable devices to monitor patients, shifts the focus from caring and healing to merely fixing problems.

The radical shift from a care-focused to a technology-focused model has also resulted in healthcare systems that operate outside the treatment facility. These systems manage and deliver health services based on a business model. The business-driven approach of healthcare systems is diminishing the importance of holistic healing. The human element in healing is replaced by bureaucracy, which is evident in data-driven healthcare systems.

In our postmodern world, medicine, treatment, and healthcare focus on "fixing" problems rather than healing. Many health professionals see it this way. In the book <u>Kitchen Table Wisdom: Stories that Heal</u>, Naomi Remen states, "When you fix, you see life as broken, but when healing and care happen, it is the work of the soul."[41] Data-driven health systems often lack a nuanced understanding of the intangible human realities that can positively impact health.

Few health providers believe that spiritual health is a relevant and meaningful way to improve health, and even fewer in the health field distinguish between the terms "spiritual" and "religious." Whether a person is healthy or not, the spiritual aspect of health is often overlooked in treatment and healthcare practices. The potential of extraordinary human experiences—exceptional spiritual experiences—to promote good health in people is underestimated.

However, in recent times, a better understanding of health is emerging. There is a resurgence in the importance placed on the spiritual aspect of health. Today, scholars, healthcare providers, professionals, and systems have started to emphasize maintaining balance in treatment. More providers and patients now value the deep human spirit, the spiritual core, the soul – or whatever term is used – as essential in treatment, healing, and maintaining good health.

Nowadays, the human spirit is increasingly emphasized in both preventive healthcare and curative treatments. The importance of this is well captured in Victor Frankl's words: "No cure that fails to engage the spirit can make us well."[42]

Present-day medical and health science researchers emphasize that the

---

[41] Remen RN, Kitchen <u>Table Wisdom: Stories that Heal</u>. Riverhead Books, 2007
[42] Frankl VE, <u>Man's Search for Meaning</u>. Beacon Press, 2006 (originally published in 1946)

"spiritual" is closely connected to people's overall health and quality of life. As the scientific community provides evidence of the spiritual component of health as a pathway to complete health, there is a reclaiming of health's deeper roots – the human spirit. We now see health treatment services focusing on spiritual health and promoting holistic health, although they have not yet distinguished between the "spiritual" and "religious" phenomena.

More relevantly, providers and patients are willing to recognize that the core reality—related to the real self or pseudo-self of a person—is producing the human spirit that deeply affects people's health. The human spirit of our times primarily reflects a blatant denial of the true self, revealing how the material focus of human nature dominates human life. This causes us to be out of touch with our daily feelings of being unsettled, disconnected, and self-alienated.

The malign human spirit in our world is not only caused by the material path of human nature controlling human life, but also influenced by the overlooked true self of people's personhood. Perhaps, this is the greatest challenge in the postmodern world for people to undertake the task of spiritual healthcare. Few realize that a map based solely on the material path of human nature guiding us in life distorts who we truly are, how we live, and what is essential to one's human life.

People experience a constant sense of self-incoherency every day. The one-dimensional nature of human existence leads to self-disintegration processes far outstripping self-integration, ultimately affecting what it means to be a person. This imbalance creates a vague sense of self that is typical of human experience. When the spiritual human nature is undermined in people's understanding of their self-reality, they often stray from the "healthy lane."

The well-adjusted, well-integrated, and "wholesome" personhood fundamentally involves the metaphysical – the non-physical human reality. The actual experience of one's human reality comes from both material and non-material aspects of human nature. Evidence from life shows that the material trajectory of human nature has caused the human person to become a soulless creature. Without the spiritual core, self-care is often neglected. There can be no proper focus on spiritual healthcare matters.

The metaphysical essence of human personhood is rooted in spiritual human nature. It helps individuals stay true to their authentic selves. What is objective and unbiased about a person is revealed through their real self. The real self inspires growth and healing. It also points to the potential of spiritual human nature to shape human life in ways that would not be possible otherwise.

Without the real self, we are tragically left with the pseudo-self to shape human life. Without the true self, people develop a functional self-concept and self-identity that hinder daily spiritual care. As a result, we can only reflect the ailing human spirit in our thoughts, feelings, and actions.

The pseudo-self undermines the metaphysical realities of human life and the higher ideals and purposes of human existence. The pseudo-self – a creation of self-fallacy ideas – has normalized ordinary people's personhood. This leads individuals to live solely by the illusions of who they believe they are and under the influence of the pseudo-self. They develop lifestyles and habits that ignore spiritual healthcare matters.

Since ancient times, humanity has believed that the metaphysical core of a person plays a key role in coexisting with the true self. Today, modern psychology suggests that the real self is the driving force in human life, expressing the metaphysical essence of personhood through the soulfulness of a person.

People's everyday self-views, feelings, and behaviors often reveal the pseudo-self. We focus on wealth, status, social power, and position as measures of human worth. Social appearance becomes more important for self-worth than the true self. The obsession with material success often masks a struggle of the human spirit, which longs for care. However, spiritual health is usually not a priority or is completely overlooked when people's attention shifts away from their inner core and the authentic self.

In today's world, we have become accustomed to living under the influence of a pseudo-self that blocks personal growth. We are constantly compelled to suppress the true self in order to gain acceptance from others. Guided by material pursuits, our lifestyles, priorities, and goals are shaped by this false self. It often appears in a self-centered way of living. People feel driven by a desire for vain glory, which is represented by material wealth, power, and self-promotion.

In our times, there is a tragic inability to distinguish the pseudo-self from the real self in everyday life. Today, external appearances are valued more than a person's true self. The desire to be authentic and to grow holistically is often ignored in the pursuit of the "good life." We overlook human virtues like wisdom, compassion, empathy, and humility, which are inherent qualities of human nature. It seems that only a rare few enlightened individuals can recognize the pseudo-self as not the true self.

In daily life, people often overlook the true value of the authentic self in healing and personal growth. The real and practical benefits of understanding how the mind works to connect with inner-core reality and staying true to the authentic self for growth, better relationships, and good health are often ignored because of utilitarian individualism, consumerism, and hedonistic values.

In our times, cultural fads and trends push people toward the pseudo-self. The material focus of human nature, by undermining the spiritual aspect, devalues the essential need for the true self in health and healing. These material influences are significantly affecting healthcare in daily life, often without people's awareness.

The wounded human spirit of our times reveals a faulty map of human nature that guides us in life. Insatiable cravings for "material excesses" and self-indulgence are turning people into bags of skin filled with deep torments, wretchedness, and brokenness. It shows what is abnormal about human nature, most affected by the dominance of material pursuits and neglecting the value of spiritual health.

Human civilization is taking a dark turn. The way we're living in the world, as a collective, is having a devastating impact on our future. We're experiencing humanity in the midst of a profound spiritual pain, with a restless and damaged human spirit. The spirit of cooperation, compassion, friendship, and love – along with deeper human connection – is eroding from human nature, bit by bit.

Utilitarian individualism and insatiable greed undermine the higher purposes of human life. They reduce human existence to a hollow pursuit of self-centered gain, resulting in emotional pain, unfulfilled desires, and the kind of spiritual wounds we see in today's society. The concept of a spiritual human nature is misguided at best and damaging at worst. The idea that religion and spiritualism can bring spiritual health is little more than wishful thinking.

The dominant cultural script pushes us toward the sensual, fleeting, mundane, and even inhumane. The "pseudo-self culture" of lies, deception, and hypocrisy destroys who we truly are and what we can become. All that is deep and sublime about human nature is less visible in everyday life. The human spirit of despair, brokenness, and misery is infecting the world and diminishing hope for a better future.

A persistent sense of turmoil, restlessness, and angst marks today's world. People are consumed by a deep-seated spirit of greed, hedonism, and all that reveals the flaws in human nature. We seem indifferent to spiritual well-being and the resulting physical, mental, and social health issues. We struggle to regulate ourselves and stay focused on higher goals. Often, people's behavior is driven by an insatiable need to satisfy their cravings and compulsions.

The quirky and fickle suffer more pain from the shifting winds of whims and fancies and have less healing through inner calm for better health. The daily choices, decisions, actions, and behaviors of ordinary people reveal the signs of a deeply wounded human spirit. Relentless hedonic cravings and existential anxiety drain the human spirit that we need to animate and uplift us.

Health researchers and experts emphasize that spiritual health is developed through the inner-core reality, which shapes a mindset to stay true to one's authentic self and to operate from the higher self. Extensive evidence from life experiences and research indicates that self-evolution and the ongoing development of personhood can energize the human spirit, providing comfort and healing.

However, regrettably, today we are becoming more accustomed to the pseudo-self and disconnected from the real self. Daily behaviors show a habitual dismissal of the true self. Our culture validates the pseudo-self as the real self. We face the consequences of our own and others' pseudo-self in families, workplaces, friendships, and almost everywhere.

Many problems in today's world are caused by people's pseudo-self. The main cause of declining physical, mental, moral, and social health is the pseudo-self. Issues like antisocial and criminal behavior highlight the pseudo-self. Despite this, society promotes a culture that encourages social masks, hypocrisy, face-saving tricks, and living a double life, all of which push us further away from our true selves. Everything about life in modern times contributes to alienating us from the inner core and authentic self.

The morbid inner-core reality and the pseudo-self are at the root of the degenerate human spirit and all human problems. It is clear in today's world that these elements create worldviews, influence life goals, and guide the life orientations of ordinary people. Only chaos can result when someone denies the inner-core reality and becomes estranged from the true self. In our time, this is evidenced by the ongoing human condition as a movement toward spiritual illness. The spiritual affliction in our world spreads like a pandemic, and its recovery remains uncertain.

In health literature, experts argue that dismissing one's inner-core reality, even casually—especially when its relevance seems blurred and purposeless—can hinder the therapeutic benefits of the true self. We often avoid confronting the true self because of the psycho-emotional stress it causes. However, ignoring the true self only worsens the human spirit within us. The battered, wounded, and suffering human spirit in our world reminds us that today, cultivating and maintaining spiritual health should be considered as urgent for healthy, high-functioning members of society as it is for those who are identified as patients, wrongdoers, or criminals.

To sum up:

The extensive health research highlights that when people enhance their spiritual health, it helps reduce negativity, stress, and anxiety, which disrupts the mind-body-spirit harmony vital for maintaining optimal health. Health researchers show that individuals who improve their spiritual health are better equipped to manage psycho-emotional conditions that harm health.[43] They provide evidence that by strengthening spiritual health, people can lessen and even eliminate the damaging effects of psycho-emotional tendencies and destructive behaviors that negatively impact healthcare outcomes.

In the health literature, spiritual health is viewed as a vital coping resource in prevention, treatment, and recovery. Health scientists identify spiritual health as an observable phenomenon and a practical construct.[44] Healthcare practitioners recommend developing lifestyles and daily routines that promote spiritual health.

Researchers demonstrate that people's spiritual health strengthens mind-oriented skills, which help build and improve psycho-emotional-behavioral pathways. They substantiate the claim that spiritual health is a key factor in enhancing overall health. They provide evidence of the "spiritual" interface with bio-psycho-social factors in establishing optimal health.[45]

---

[43] Ballew SH, Hannum SM, Gaines JM, Marx KA, Parrish JM, The Role of Spiritual Experiences and Activities in the Relationship between Chronic Illness and Psychological Well-being. Journal of Religion and Health (Vol 51) 2012

[44] Ganbhari R and Mohammedimehr, Identification of Dimensions and Indicators of Spiritual Health: A Qualitative Study. Journal of Education and Health Promotion, December 2020

[45] Balboni, VanderWeele, Koh, et al. Spirituality in Serious Illness and Health. JAMA, July 2022

Overall, research so far has shown that spiritual health generally reduces sickness and disease and promotes holistic health and living.

Medical science affirms that the physical, mental, and social components of health depend on the spiritual component of health. It recognizes that the spiritual component helps reduce numerous harmful influences on physical and mental health. Researchers provide evidence that spiritual health has beneficial effects on reducing levels of the stress hormone, thereby enhancing the positive experience of health conditions in people. The documented evidence demonstrates that spiritual health offers salutary effects on cardiovascular disease, blood pressure, the nervous system, and the immune system.

Health sciences claim that good health is achieved through the intermediary of psycho-emotional-behavioral pathways. Today, the treatment of mental disorders, substance abuse, sexual disorders, and suicidal behaviors increasingly relies on patients' spiritual health. The evidence in research literature consistently shows the benefits of spiritual health across various populations and health measures.

People often overlook the advantages of developing spiritual health. It does not receive the attention it deserves in efforts to improve overall health. Little consideration is given to the potential of spiritual human nature to unlock and encourage healing benefits across all areas of life. Few are aware of the scientific evidence supporting the positive effects of maintaining spiritual health.

Today, preventive health care is prioritized over curative health care. Growing spiritual health is seen as an effective way to stay proactive in preventive health. We gain insights and wisdom to focus on what enhances and hinders good health in everyday life.

Importantly, people's spiritual health is gaining recognition in efforts to heal both humanity and the planet. Spiritual health is not only a crucial aspect of medicine, treatment, and personal care but also essential for the well-being of humanity and Earth. Experts view it as vital for restoring the holistic human being and promoting a holistic way of life. Furthermore, it is argued that humanity's health is at risk when individuals neglect self-evolution to become "whole" and develop psychosocial maturity to face challenges in human life in the postmodern world.

Today, we often overlook the ripple effects that health has on others. Few consider healthcare as the primary human vocation, and even fewer realize that health is never solely about the individual but also about the collective. An individual's good or poor health affects others, and their healthcare habits need to be aimed not only at personal well-being but also at benefiting society, humanity, and the planet. In this way, each of us has a responsibility to promote good health for all. Developing spiritual health is a positive way to support the well-being of individuals, society, and humanity at the same time.

HOW TO NURTURE SPIRITUAL HEALTH

We have already seen that the "spiritual" and "religious" phenomena are different. We know the "religious way of life" is a cultural addition, and spiritual health depends on the development of human consciousness and self-evolution. We have also learned that neuroscience shows neurobiological processes are involved in "spiritual experiences" that foster spiritual health. Neuroscientists have provided evidence for the neural basis of spiritual human nature and the neurobiological foundations of spiritual health.

One's spiritual health is not something ethereal or influenced by celestial powers but an essential part of human existence, health, and growth. It results from the intentional effort to live fully with all aspects of human nature, to grow in completeness, and to develop a healthy way of life.

The cultivation of spiritual health is always intentional, meaning it involves recalibrating the imagination and willpower to help the whole person grow, ultimately benefiting society and creating a healthier humanity. Experiencing "wholeness" within oneself and living in a "wholesome" way represent the experience of spiritual health. This is reflected in the better version of one's personhood exhibited in everyday life. People's sense of spiritual health emerges through the human qualities of self-transcendence and being other-oriented.

Firstly, spiritual health is a result of the development of an individual's human consciousness and self-growth. It comes from resolving deeper issues related to the inner core reality that negatively impacts the true self of a person's identity. The pseudo-self is overcome when one achieves high levels of spiritual health. This is reflected in the holistic person and a holistic way of living.

Growing spiritual health requires us to stay aware of the mind's processes during real-time life experiences and focus on self-evolution to stay true to our authentic selves. This is the main work involved in developing and maintaining spiritual health. Implicit in growing and maintaining spiritual health are the "renewing" and "becoming" processes of the individual. These processes result from the focus placed on one's spiritual nature to actualize the "whole" human person and promote a "wholesome" way of life.

Spiritual health results from a synergistic interaction among everyday life processes, a person's developing human consciousness, and self-evolution. Ordinary life experiences form the foundation on which spiritual health is built and sustained. The growth of human consciousness and a person's self-evolution occur within the realm of everyday life. Self-evolution always depends on the progression of human consciousness.

The journey to a "healthy me" is always a deeply personal endeavor. It's hard work that must be done and cannot be avoided, and the responsibility for it rests solely with me. Others can never do it for us. Each person must put together the pieces of the "me" and create the "wholeness" needed to move toward a "healthy me." The journey to a "healthy me" is never-ending.

There is no single approach to developing spiritual health. The journey to a "healthy me" always involves each person's unique traits and life circumstances, along with overcoming psycho-emotional obstacles and challenges specific to the individual. Furthermore, there is a need to commit to the "spiritual laws" of nature. Practically, this means adhering to "spiritual principles" and engaging in "spiritual practices" that support the growth of optimal health. Today, there are time-tested, verifiable spiritual principles and evidence-based spiritual practices—distinct from the gimmicks often found in the spiritual marketplace—that are proven to facilitate the evolution of human consciousness and promote self-growth.

The cultivation of spiritual health is naturally aimed at the development of human consciousness. As human consciousness evolves, it allows us to explore more deeply who we are, what our purpose is, and where we are heading in life. It clarifies who a person truly is and who they are not. The true self is distinguished from the false self and takes priority over it.

The best reflection of a person's spiritual health is the positive impact of evolving human consciousness on their personhood. A flourishing personhood is demonstrated through virtues, consistent soulfulness, a noble way of life, and a strong sense of shared humanity. One shows the superiority of human nature in the natural world through "spiritual selfhood." Being a truly "alive" human in any situation is not automatic but depends on one's level of spiritual health.

As people evolve in human consciousness, it helps reduce self-centered thoughts and behaviors, and what genuinely matters to human life and existence becomes a priority in daily choices and decisions. A higher level of human consciousness in a person creates perspectives and perceptions that differ from the default consciousness – also called ordinary or waking consciousness – emphasizing high-mindedness, virtue, and dedication to the common good.

Neuroscience emphasizes that higher levels of human consciousness enhance cognitive functions, fostering intuition, insightfulness, and sensory perception that expand perspectives to see and experience life in new ways. The inherent "spiritual capacities" of human nature emerge daily. Experts in human consciousness suggest that as our consciousness evolves, we develop positive personality traits and grow in human qualities, demonstrating the consistency of holistic personhood.

Neuroscience shows that positive changes occur in brain chemistry, mechanisms, and functions as people advance in human consciousness.[46] These changes enhance a person's cognitive and emotional abilities, making them richer and better. When people operate from higher levels of consciousness, they reveal the "extraordinary" potential within the "ordinary" human organism. Experiencing high levels of spiritual health demonstrates that the "extraordinary" human organism is a dormant potential that anyone can actualize intentionally.

Usually, we are not present in the here and now and don't truly experience life as it unfolds. We aren't tuned into the inner workings of the mind. The static human consciousness—default consciousness—generally limits thoughts, perspectives, and sensory perceptions regarding ourselves, others, and the world around us.

Modern health sciences provide scientific evidence of "spiritual practices" that effectively eliminate the blurring effect of fiction and reality in daily life. These practices help deepen awareness of the present moment and the inner core of one's self and human existence as life unfolds. They have been shown to help people overcome the "pseudo self," bridge the "actual self" and the "real self," and cultivate the "higher self."

Every day, we navigate life with unresolved issues related to the inner-core reality within ourselves and others. This results from the unchanging, static human consciousness. It hinders our inherent "spiritual capacities" like intuition and insight, and limits the perspectives and perceptions that foster self-evolution. Static human consciousness strongly indicates the neglected inner-core reality and true self, as well as the disregard for one's spiritual health.

The unchanging human consciousness predicts potential personal health issues, unethical and deviant behaviors, malicious activities, violence,

---

[46] Ashbrook JB, Albright CR, The Humanizing Brain: Where Religion and Neuroscience Meet. Pilgrim Press 1997

social unrest, and geopolitical tensions. In today's way of being human, the true self is often overlooked within a person's reality, even unknowingly. The default human consciousness—static and unchanging—stabilizes the pseudo-self, making it seem like the real self to us.

Essentially, developing spiritual health revolves around one's inner core reality, staying true to the authentic self, and recognizing the ultimate human nature. It concerns the most unique, constant, and enduring relationship one will ever have in life—a relationship with "me." It also involves carrying this relationship into the broader world. The connection with the "real me" will never be hidden, overshadowed, or diminished within the overall human experience of personhood.

In today's world, the way of being human often involves carelessly ignoring our true selves and willingly accepting false ideas about who we are. Our lifestyle is solely shaped by a culture that promotes the pseudo-self. We imitate traits and tendencies of this false self, as pushed by the media, advertisements, and internet culture. Additionally, the culture of individualism, materialism, and hedonism encourages values, attitudes, and priorities that reinforce the illusions of our true identity.

At the same time, deep within our thoughts, we mourn who we pretend to be and are not. Each day, we struggle to manage the agitation of the restless human spirit we carry with us. We endure a mind that is never steady, balanced, or clear in objective truth. We are overwhelmed by insurmountable stressors and self-destructive tendencies. We feel disjointed inside and outside. We are disoriented by a diffused sense of meaning and purpose in our human life. We fight not to be overtaken by psycho-somatic factors that underpin health issues. We are overwhelmed and desperate for solutions to the grave problems facing humanity. We seek relief from chaotic conditions in our world, from existential angst, and from hopeless despair.

Today, in many different ways and moments across life's experiences, a recurring question often arises in people's minds: Why do I do what I do? Or, how can I shift my human consciousness? We strive for the "healthy me" and crave a more revitalized human spirit. We seek clarity about who we truly are and the real meaning of human life. We experience countless fleeting moments when we long for a more regenerative human spirit – it is a desire for spiritual health!

Today, more people turn to modern health science to understand how to cultivate spiritual health in ways that transcend the boundaries of any religion or religious doctrine. A large body of scholars and resources explores the "spiritual phenomenon" as distinct from the "religious phenomenon,' leading to a better understanding of our innate "spiritual capacities.' Scientific knowledge about spiritual health offers new perspectives on health, emphasizing the benefits of holistic well-being. People are increasingly dedicating time and effort to developing their spiritual health. Evidence-based practices are being sought to nurture and enhance spiritual health.

Today, we live in a world where the level of human consciousness in each other is less overlooked and better recognized. The evolved or higher level of human consciousness is now distinguished from the ordinary default consciousness. The evolved, transformed, and advanced state of human consciousness is evident in people who positively influence the world around them. They demonstrate comprehensive life perspectives and worldviews, along with higher-order thinking, values, priorities, drives, and behaviors. It highlights the positive effects of engaging with life through spiritual human nature and nurturing spiritual health.

The staggering statistics on high rates of crime, suicide, and homicide, as well as overcrowded mental health facilities and prisons, courtroom dramas, and widespread antisocial behaviors, reveal severely disturbed states of human consciousness in today's world. It is recognized through psychological imbalances, painful experiences of self-disintegration, the epidemic of character disorders, and a malfunctioning human society. The withered, wounded, and weakened human spirit highlights the experience of lower levels of human consciousness in people. The degenerated humanity, the corrupt human person, and the dehumanized human life in our world plainly reflect the current state of humanity's consciousness.

For many centuries, religion created a deep and false divide between science and the phenomenon of spiritual health. However, modern medicine and the health sciences demonstrate that they are not only compatible but also essential.

In our times, the science of human health – rather than religion – is proving to be more relevant and useful in cultivating and maintaining spiritual health. Modern health science shows that spiritual health does not come from a jumble of prayer formulas, belief systems, and religious rituals. It is not some magical event that happens in religion or spiritualism, or through products sold in the "spiritual marketplace."

Modern health sciences recognize the human brain as the material and efficient cause of spiritual health. They emphasize the psychological and neurological basis on which spiritual health is built. Neuroscience shows that non-ordinary human experiences – "exceptional spiritual experiences" – induce positive changes in brain mechanisms and chemistry to develop the "spiritual brain" and enhance spiritual health.

Neuroscience shows there is a neural basis for human consciousness. It emphasizes the human brain as both the receiver and transmitter of consciousness. Neuroscientists have demonstrated that neurological processes and endocrine systems work together to regulate, coordinate, and enhance levels of human consciousness.

The human brain can respond to positive and negative life influences in many ways. What neuroscience is clarifying is that we have the ability to intentionally change brain functions to influence consciousness. The human brain can be trained to operate in a way that supports deliberate and purposeful living. The potential of human brain systems to develop human consciousness gives a person the ability to reorient themselves in the world.

Neuroscience indicates an inherent neurobiological potential to enhance the human mind, allowing a person to live more effectively, intentionally, and purposefully. The brain can improve cognitive, psycho-emotional, and behavioral abilities to enrich human life. Modern health sciences have studied specific "spiritual practices," supporting people's non-ordinary human experiences—exceptional spiritual experiences—that are known to positively alter neurological processes and endocrine systems, thereby affecting human consciousness and boosting one's "spiritual condition"—spiritual health.

Health sciences offer evidence-based "spiritual techniques" and highlight that developing spiritual health involves essential self-evolution to stay true to the authentic self, which is seen as the driving force of life. Health scientists and researchers connect the evolution of human consciousness and self-growth with spiritual health. Health practitioners focus on self-awareness, self-regulation, and self-transcendence to foster spiritual health.

What the health industry needs to emphasize more is that spiritual health is a part of human health, and one must be intentional and purposeful in developing spiritual health. This is no different from intentionally and purposefully building physical, mental, or social health.

"Spiritual technologies," as described by some health scientists and experts, are gaining popularity and thriving in our current times. These technologies are demonstrating numerous benefits for human consciousness, self-evolution, and overall health. Spiritual technologies are revealing that an intriguing path is opening between the scientific and spiritual worlds.

The author has identified in the health science literature evidence-based spiritual technologies and time-tested, verifiable spiritual principles that support the evolution of consciousness and enable the true self to become an active force in life. These are strongly emphasized by experts in the field and the scientific community and are widely recognized for their positive effects on health and spiritual well-being. They are:

Deliberate Pace of Life

First, spiritual health can be affected by something as simple as how fast life moves. Usually, people don't realize that the speed at which they live can influence them spiritually. Health sciences highlight this as an important factor in maintaining well-being.

The journey to a "healthy me" is a moment-by-moment experience. It involves the complex inner workings of the human body that are present in everyday moments as life unfolds. It is about being aware of the map of one's human nature, guiding and shaping life in the present. It is the endless discovery in current moments of what truly makes us human and how to develop the "whole" human person.

The journey to a "healthy me" is about being fully "present" in each current moment. Some call it "essential awareness" or "mindfulness." It involves paying attention to your inner mental processes in the here and now. We accept the "as-is" self of the present moment to stay true to our authentic selves. We avoid getting distracted by rigid ideas of who we are, were, or will become.

Instead, we focus on the inner-core and existential realities. It requires us to detach from the reality that exists only in the mind. This calls us to "switch off" the autopilot mode of distraction from the present moment.

Today, almost everyone suffers from the "hurrying sickness" in society. We constantly miss the present moment. Modern society as a whole is rushing to make everything faster. The hurried, restless, frantic way of life each day feels like an almost incurable illness in the world. Nearly everyone believes that speeding up life is unavoidable.

The "hurrying sickness" in modern-day society is a sign of imbalance in human life today. It leads to harmful thinking and behavior patterns that affect how we live. We seem unable to recognize that the constantly rushing and fast-paced life creates disease in the body, mind, and spirit, and is the root of many human problems in our times.

Arguably, preventing all forms of illness and disease is the most reliable way to meet our health needs. The present moment is when we stop poor health from occurring. A healthy society and humanity grow when people are alert, aware, and fully alive as life unfolds in every present moment.

Health literature reveals that people experience in everyday life the harmful effects of a fast-paced lifestyle. These include shallow breathing, feeling tired yet wired, poor sleep patterns, difficulty relaxing, sugar cravings, recurring headaches, irritability, mood swings, digestive issues, poor short-term memory, and more. People often find it easier to turn to medication for the unexpected consequences of a hectic life rather than changing their pace of living.

In health science literature, researchers reveal that when people increase their pace of life, workload, and "life load," they also elevate metabolic arousal to levels that negatively and seriously impact health.[47] Moreover, the tyranny of the accelerated speed of life creates distorted perceptions, sterilizes communications, and deprives people of the aesthetic texture of human life.

Researchers report that the cost of "speed addiction" in our society has led to a concerning increase in various stress-related disorders across all ages.[48] Health experts say that the overstimulation from the fast pace of life is causing everyday mood, attention, and behavioral issues, which have serious effects on physical and mental health, as well as contributing to violence, crime, and other social problems.

The most common reason for "speed addiction" is the belief that slowing down means falling behind in life. Usually, human life is driven by the basic need for security and self-preservation. When looked at closely, habitual rushing mainly comes from how a person seeks security and self-preservation. It all depends on how the individual defines success and happiness.

---

[47] Warf B, Teaching Time-Space Compression. J. Geogr. Higher Educ., 35 (2) 2011.
[48] Brown S, Speed: Facing our Addiction to Fast and Faster – and Overcoming our Fear of Slowing Down. Berkley Books, 2014

Many scholars believe that the rapid pace of life creates daily experiences of stress, leading to self-alienation and psycho-emotional instability.[49] Increased busyness in our times not only causes physical exhaustion and mental fatigue but also reduces people's ability for deeper self-awareness, intuition, and sensory perception. Many are unaware of the underlying harmful psychology that raises their risk of engaging in problematic and criminal behaviors. Hospitals, mental health facilities, courtrooms, and prisons illustrate a rise in incidents of acting out that are later regretted.

In postmodern times, the global cultural trend of the "go-faster world" reflects a form of technological determinism in people's thinking. Today's world is propelled by an apparently intentional speed of technological processes. The rapid pace of life created by internet culture has become irresistible to ordinary people and seems unavoidable and essential in human existence. Every day, it makes people feel powerless to control the pace of life, affecting the fundamental aspects of health and happiness. It took a pandemic for us to realize the "go-faster world" we've created and to confront the serious consequences it has on the quality of human life.

The COVID-19 pandemic created a "global pause time" and helped people become more aware of the dangers and problems resulting from the momentum of the postmodern world. In many ways, the lockdown made people everywhere realize they had never been as happy, fulfilled, or healthy as they were during that time. However, for some people, the lockdown had harmful effects such as mental health issues, substance abuse, and suicide. This is most likely because the previously dismissed true self became overwhelming in their awareness, as never before.

Besides, during the "global pause time," people vividly experienced in real time what a more natural world and normal humanity looked like – how a less hurried world positively affected all of human life. For example, the

---

[49] Wajcman J and Dodd N. (Eds.) The Sociology of Speed: Digital, Organization, and Social Temporalities. Oxford University Press, 2016

lockdown allowed people to see the environmental benefits of reducing carbon emissions. They became aware of the adverse effects of the faster pace of living on daily life. Sadly, that awareness now seems fleeting, as we continue to prioritize health and well-being in the same way we did before the pandemic.

The collateral damage of a fast-paced lifestyle is the limited time people have for themselves. When caught up in the turbulence of reckless speed in life, we tend also to find ourselves in a turbulent inner world. Chronic speed has delirious effects on our sense of self. It causes us to develop a cognitive quirk called self-fallacy – pseudo-self. The pseudo-self is a side effect of people caught up in the fast pace of life.

People are overwhelmed by the fast pace of life to the point of losing self-awareness and self-understanding. Perhaps, in today's world, the most critical goal for growth, health, and happiness is to achieve an intentional speed of life that promotes self-animation. We need a deliberate pace of life that energizes the mind, body, and spirit, and fosters internal and external harmony. There is a pressing need to control the speed of one's life better to enhance health, well-being, and happiness.

The cultural obsession with productivity and material prosperity is a relentless grind. It underlies many of our health problems, but, more importantly, it hampers inward reflection. As addictive inner pressure and chronic stress become more common in our way of life, we self-alienate to the point of self-sabotage. This can be seen every day in the harm done to optimal health, the best version of ourselves, and our dysfunctional relationship patterns.

There is an urgent need to live in sync with the pace of life to better align with human nature on a metaphysical level. In today's global culture, we navigate life with a distorted understanding of human nature and are indifferent to our epistemological perspectives. We desperately need greater attentiveness to incorporate the metaphysical realities of human nature so we can engage more meaningfully and effectively in life.

In a world where productivity and achievement are prioritized, self-awareness is the first step toward redefining what productivity and achievement truly mean for us. Self-awareness can help us reevaluate critical issues and choices, fostering a holistic way of living. It can lead us to change internalized values and become more open to the inherent potential to build a cohesive self, which a healthier humanity depends on. Through self-awareness, we can be more intentional with the pace of life for deeper self-understanding and personal growth, ultimately enhancing health and society's welfare.

Modern health science links self-awareness to positive psychological well-being. In health literature, it is seen as a key way to reduce psychological distress and promote self-growth. Researchers differentiate between dispositional self-awareness (mindful living) and situational self-awareness (self-reflection moments), highlighting that dispositional self-awareness leads to greater positive effects on personal well-being.

Self-awareness has become the latest buzzword in healthcare—and for good reason. Researchers show that when we see ourselves clearly, we make better decisions, build stronger relationships, and live more fulfilling lives.[50] Although many believe they are self-aware, studies reveal that accurate self-awareness is a rare trait. In the research literature, it is suggested that only about 10 to 15 percent of people have the ability for dispositional self-awareness.

Self-awareness can be difficult in a culture that promotes the pseudo-self. Research shows that when people feel trapped outside of self-awareness—unable to access unconscious thoughts, feelings, and motives—they tend to believe the ideas they create about who they are. The pseudo-self is often mistaken for the real self.

Every day, essential awareness and dispositional self-awareness help a person become alert to what truly matters in life and to imbalances in all parts of human existence. This often acts as a gateway to the spiritual dimension of

---

[50] Tasha E. Insight: Why We're Not As Self-aware As We Think, And How Seeing Ourselves Clearly Helps Us Succeed At Work and In Life. Currency Press, 2017

life. People recognize the importance of the spiritual dimension by moving toward understanding what the fast pace of life and the rush of the postmodern world mean for health, sanity, and humanity.

To nurture spiritual health, people should start with something as simple as finding the right pace of life. Experts say there is a natural rhythm in the universe.[51] They believe that, as part of the natural world order, humans need to adjust to this rhythm. It is thought that when we are in harmony with the natural rhythm, life flows smoothly; when we are out of sync, it leads to many challenges and problems in our human experience.

In today's world, nearly everyone succumbs to the out-of-control pace of life. It's always a struggle to stay in the here-and-now moment. The old patterns and fixed ideas of the mind want to repeat. There is always a compulsion to control and force things to happen. It is tough to "let be" or "let go." However, to learn and be guided by lived experiences, one must stay present. We need to adapt to life's natural rhythm.

For almost everyone, the rush of life becomes a distraction from the true self. When we're not in the present moment, we're poorly self-aware. We overlook the inner processes of the mind that help us understand the effects of the core inner reality. We are disconnected from the "as-is" self-reality – the real self. We only begin to align with the natural rhythm of life when we prioritize the "inner world" and the true self.

The true self is always a present-moment self-reality – the here-and-now "real me." We connect with the here-and-now real me through inward attention that depends on the pace of life. There is always so much that is overlooked about the real me when someone is driven by outward attention. This is no different than what happens when someone drives a vehicle at a very high speed. Details get missed!

The intentional pace of life is designed to support the executive

---

[51] Circadian Rhythms Fact Sheet, 2012. Retrieved from NIGMS website

function of the real self. At every moment, either the real self or the pseudo-self guides how we live. Both the real self and pseudo-self are fundamental human experiences and significantly influence our way of living. The real self serves as a motivating force in human life, fostering personal growth and happiness. To live intentionally, we must recognize the valuable role of the real self in healing, maturity, inner security, and joy.

Today, in the rush to satisfy a superficial human existence, the true self is not distinguished from the person who is driven to acquire, possess, and accumulate external things in life. What is real and the mental image of what is real are indistinguishable. People are trapped in a single static frame within the constant flow of life, like a frozen frame of a film.

The deliberate pace of life is designed to help us distinguish the true self from the actual self or pseudo-self. When the true self is not separated from the actual self or pseudo-self, it sets the stage for a range of problems in one's life. In every present moment, a person has the opportunity to transition from the actual self or pseudo-self to the true self.

The practice of intentionally slowing down life helps us face many personal and life truths that we may have avoided, intentionally or unintentionally. It fosters awareness of our true selves and helps us hold onto our personal truth and reality. When people recognize the forces of the world—such as those damaging health, relationships, "wholeness" of personhood, and hindering a soulful life—they begin to breathe, live, and stay awake and alert.

When authentic to one's true self, there are fewer instincts driven by pressure and haste, and more instincts rooted in simply being. Consequently, productivity, achievement, self-understanding, and self-acceptance are not dictated by external standards. The fast pace of life is understood for what it truly is – detrimental to the vibrant, soulful, holistic human experience.

The "hurrying sickness" in society is unique to the postmodern world and represents a magnetic pull away from more meaningful participation in life. When caught in this societal hurrying sickness, the energizing force within a person is subdued and stifled. In health literature, slowing down is seen as the key to improving personal health, as well as fostering a healthier humanity and a healthier planet.

To sum up:

In our time, the speed of human life is unlike any other in history. It is at extremes never before seen. Anthropologists tell us that our pre-agrarian ancestors worked as little as four hours a day and slept twice daily. For them, everyday life focused on survival needs. But since humans realized the need to generate surpluses, the pace of life has never stopped speeding up. Technological progress through the centuries has not only improved human life but also increased the pace of life to the level we experience today.

Today, people often face a world filled with endless distractions that block self-truths and life-truths. They constantly experience the human mind as a pile of mental clutter marked by confusion and conflicts. It is full of ways to avoid taking responsibility for the present moment. The automatic repetition of old mental patterns dominates how they think, feel, and behave.

The addiction to speed is a constant obstacle to inward attention. The present moment always seems to vanish in endless distractions between the past and the future. The intricate mechanism of our deeper feelings and emotions makes detecting them one of life's greatest challenges. We desperately need a pace of life that sharpens the mind to deeper feelings, emotions, and impulses, and also makes us more alert to reactivity in thoughts and behaviors.

The momentum of our postmodern world causes cognitive and sensory overloads. Our ability to concentrate and focus often declines or is completely lost. For some people, even many traditional techniques for staying calm, focused, and present are no longer effective. The capacity to be aware and live in the moment has weakened or seems impossible for many. Still, inward awareness and being in the here-and-now are essential to prevent the endless stream of thoughts, emotions, impulses, and drives from controlling our lives.

The present moment always offers clarity, harmony, and stability for us. Awareness in the present acts as the antidote to the habit of experiencing life as constantly filled with pressures, urgencies, and emergencies. Awareness is like "taking a break in time" from the hyper-arousal of rushing forward habits, to create a "mental space" to be "fully alive" to life as it unfolds.

The intentional pace of life is primarily about maintaining the ability to choose the life we want to live, a power to be free from mental and emotional clutter, a power to "live free" and be "fully alive." This is the power of "now" that brings inner freedom and psychological-emotional stability in each present moment. When we approach the present with curiosity, we discover new insights about ourselves and gain new perspectives.

The work involved in building spiritual health takes place in every present moment, whether a person is acting well or poorly, doing right or wrong, experiencing pain or pleasure. The psychological awareness formed offers clear, honest, and realistic views and perspectives that focus on the whole human person and a holistic way of living. In this way, it is in the present moment that we create and sustain spiritual health—by growing and maintaining it.

Living in the present moment is the first step we take to cultivate, recover, and maintain spiritual health. Awareness shows us that the present is eternal and the only true eternity in life. This is an undeniable truth of human life, and we can all learn to accept it. When we do, we choose a pace in life that energizes and revitalizes the human spirit.

The deliberate pace in life that energizes the human spirit fosters natural healing in every part of human life. We live free from automatic subconscious destructive thoughts and behaviors. Healing occurs by letting go of unrealistic standards and impossible ideals used to judge and condemn ourselves or others. It happens when we avoid habits of the mind that lead to self-sabotage. It comes from empathy and tolerance for all of our human flaws, weaknesses, and foolishness. It results from showing tenderness to ourselves by not being stuck in a fixed state of life.

The deliberate pace of life gives us every present moment to embrace our true selves and all fact-based experiences that are normal to human nature. What happens in the present moment is not ignored or hidden, even if it is seen as terrible or evil. There is unconditional acceptance of one's human fragility and steadfast perseverance in the effort to become the whole human being capable of. Each present moment is like a tiny history because it is also a broad view – the intersection of one's past and future. It's as if every page of one's human life story is written in the present moment. This is a real-life story that includes endless experiences of joy and pain, despair and suffering, love and rejection, success and loss, and all the extremes of human life. In that story, no human experience is denied, no matter how it is judged or condemned.

Health sciences highlight the many physical, mental, psychological, and spiritual benefits gained from dispositional awareness in daily life.[52] The human mind, in the present moment, is always the gateway to unlimited possibilities. A fast-paced life subjects the human mind to chaotic entropy, hindering exponential personal growth and health. The chaos within a person weakens the "renewal energy" of the human organism. Neuroscience views the chaotic flow of bio-energy patterns in the human body as neurophysiological disintegrations. Experts argue that chaotic bio-energy patterns in the human body contribute to health issues today.[53]

The entropic effect of a fast-paced life negatively impacts people's bio-energy fields. Negative bio-energy fields in individuals create a pathogenic energy field in the world. Some experts believe that the accelerated pace of our

---

[52] Carver C S, Self-awareness (2003) in Leary M R & Tangney J P (Eds.) HandBook of Self and Identity. Guilford.
Grant A M, Franklin J, and Langford P. The Self-reflection and Insight Scale: A New Measure of Private Self-Consciousness. Social Behavior and Personality: An International Journal (8) (2002).
[53] Hufford D, Sprengel M, et.al. Barriers to the Entry of Biofield Healing into "Mainstream" Healthcare. Glob Adv Health Med (4) 2015

world hinders the "renewal energy" and "salutogenic energy" fields in human life today.

The world today desperately needs the calm, healing human spirit. It can be as contagious as the restlessness we constantly observe around us. Composed and focused individuals influence positive change in others. The soothing and revitalizing human spirit serves as an antidote to the broken and wounded spirit that is widespread in our world.

The challenges and problems in human life are closely linked to losing the present moment. Living at a deliberate pace helps people regain balance when they feel off, or as the French say, "nous ne sommes pas dans nos assiettes," meaning, "we are not in our plates," or "we are out of sorts."

Meditation

This is an age of self-alienation, multitasking, and poor attention span. We experience an overload of information, sensations, and confusion. Individually and collectively, we are filled with uncertainty, stress, loneliness, anxiety, grief, fear, depression, anger, insecurity, restlessness, frustration, hopelessness, and much more. The average person's mind is cluttered with mental debris. Nearly everyone struggles with a restless, agitated, chaotic mind and feels overwhelmed by internal stress.

The typical mind of an average person is chaotic, cluttered, or fragmented. Researchers say that the human mind produces over fifty to seventy thousand thoughts daily. In literature, experts compare the human mind to a jittery, chattering monkey. They call it "monkey mind" because it resists any attempt to be tamed or to stay quiet. The "monkey-mind syndrome" describes the human mind as tending to be restless, constantly preoccupied, difficult to control, and sometimes causing people to behave like an aggressive volcano.

Being human right now means feeling the urge to escape the present moment. To do so, we have adopted various forms of denial, numbing, and distraction. Throughout the day, many rely on chemicals and technology to alter their mood and mind. More people find themselves obsessively "partying" and playing video games to relieve the stress caused by their thoughts. To make matters worse, an "attention-hogging" device has embedded itself into our pockets. This has caused the human mind today to constantly "want more" and to look "out there."

For many people in our world, it is nearly impossible to simply be quiet, still, centered, and focused. We have a strong need to escape from the burdensome mind. This is probably also why, unlike any previous generations, we are constantly on the move—jet-setters and global travelers—covering great distances to find wonderlands. However, few realize that they may change the sky but not the mind.

However, all our numbing and distraction do not solve the problem. Instead, it only worsens, as shown by how life unfolds in modern society. This is evident in the increasing issues related to physical, mental, and social health, the widespread malaise of drug abuse and dependence, violent crimes, and the staggering statistics on suicides and homicides in communities worldwide.

An ordinary person's mind almost always focuses outward. Everything in the external world competes for attention. Whether deliberate or not, we often neglect the rich inner world. In a world that continually increases cognitive and sensory overloads, people rarely feel drawn to inward attention or to the awareness of life as it unfolds. Few are willing to become aware of the inner processes of the mind. Even fewer are willing to fight the battle against escaping the present moment and developing inward attention. Still, even fewer have the discipline and focus to stand against denial, numbness, and distraction.

What modern health science recognizes and shows is that the "monkey-mind syndrome" negatively affects the psycho-emotional states that cause all the imbalances in life. Today, the restlessness of the human mind creates dangerous levels of stress in people. Health experts argue that internal stressors are harder to manage than external ones. For example, we can more easily control external stressors like environmental noise by moving to a new home, but when we brood over something, it is difficult to control the internal stress it creates. Some in the scientific community see the "monkey-mind syndrome" as a weapon of mass destruction.

Everyone longs to go beyond the limits set by the mind. The "monkey-mind syndrome" highlights the essential human need to stay centered, aware, and focused. This occurs when the mind is trained to remain in the present moment and stay connected with its inner processes. For the millions around the world, practicing meditation daily proves helpful in achieving this. Many people, by meditating daily, enhance their dispositional awareness, self-awareness, and much more.

Research on meditation shows that daily practice removes the constant flow of thoughts and emotions. It helps individuals become non-reactive, calm, peaceful, receptive, and attentively aware. This has led neuroscience experts to view meditation as the brain's discipline center, where the "monkey mind" is tamed to stay in the present moment. Extensive scientific evidence demonstrates that meditation enhances concentration, attention span, awareness, and self-regulation. Meditation balances the tendency to focus outwardly and overlook the rich inner world.

In meditation, the human mind is trained through disciplined practice of centering and focusing—discipline and concentration—to maintain full attention on the present moment. The intricate mechanisms of the human brain are designed to support awareness, focus, and self-regulation, preventing the mind from drifting away from the present moment. This enhances the unique ability of the human mind to be aware of being aware and to think about thinking.

The fundamental drive of the human body is to maintain homeostasis and survive. Meditation is proven to positively affect the brain mechanisms that support homeostasis. It has a calming and healing effect on the biological body. Meditation fosters calmness and balance, enhancing the body's functioning. Health science supports the idea that daily meditation practice is central to renewing energy flow in the body and effectively improving mental well-being. The changes in brain mechanisms and chemicals caused by practice are shown to benefit overall health.

According to neuroscience, daily meditation is a powerful tool for rewiring the brain and tapping into the mind's potential for balance and calm.[54] Research in modern psychology shows that meditation can significantly improve cognitive and emotional functions.[55] Regular practice leads to greater mental clarity, better emotional balance, and a more stable sense of self. Meditation also helps people stay focused in the midst of life and live more in the present.

Experts say that practicing meditation daily helps people shift from a cluttered mind to a more intuitive one.[56] Meditation refines the human mind to focus on the core and experience of universality. Many find that meditation helps remove misperceptions, turns off the mind's focus on the past and future, and enables them to go beyond the chaos and overstimulation of the world.

Typically, the purpose and meaning of life are small glimpses within each person, rooted in basic thoughts, feelings, and actions, but they are also intertwined with the instinct to survive. Usually, people search for life's purpose and meaning through their mind's fantasies in pursuit of happiness. We desire happiness in things that are temporary and often overlook the fleeting nature of all things, including human life itself. For thousands of years, meditation has helped people become unburdened by a "passing world" and foster a "sense of self" that is healthier, more transparent, and more secure in all relationships.

Meditation helps people connect with deeper feelings and emotions, becoming more comfortable with their unique psychological makeup. They are

---

[54] Fox KCR, Nijeboer S, Dixon ML, et al. Is Meditation Associated With Altered Brain Structure? A Systematic Review and Meta-Analysis of Morphometric Neuroimaging in Meditation Practitioners. Neuroscience & Biobehavioral Reviews 2014
[55] Keng SL, Smoski MJ, Robins CJ Effects of Mindfulness on Psychological Health: A Review of Empirical Studies. Clinical Psychology Rev 2011
[56] Eberth J and Sedlmeier P The Effects of Mindfulness Meditation: A Meta-Analysis. Mindfulness. May 2012

less distracted from their true self, which makes them more grounded, focused, and confident when facing life's unpredictability, challenges, and threats. People find that meditation empowers them to live from their depths and engage in life with higher ideals and purposes.

Mediation helps people develop inner calm and heal from the frantic spirit caused by restless minds. Those who meditate daily embody a way of living that is soulful. The compassion, higher purposes, inclusive thinking, and other-oriented behaviors they bring into the world highlight the transformed self—a "new self" with the higher-order thinking and behaviors of a "higher self." Many people find that meditation restores transcendence in life, which is essential for being true to the metaphysical essence of human nature.

Research shows that daily meditation benefits human consciousness. People who meditate every day tend to operate from an altered or non-ordinary state of consciousness, different from the usual static default. Environmental triggers and impulses have less influence on them. They gain deeper insights, perceptions, intuition, and practical wisdom, allowing them to go beyond surface-level understanding. As a result, they grow in self-knowledge and self-awareness, fostering personal evolution.

Overall, meditation is a valuable resource for human health and growth that can promote positive change in the world. Medical science views meditation as a simple and effective way to reduce stress and aid the body's internal healing process. Modern psychology finds that meditation enhances self-awareness and self-regulation, helping people move away from automatic, unconscious reactions internally and externally. Human consciousness literature states that meditation transforms human consciousness, expanding the horizons of human life.

There have been over three thousand scientific studies on meditation since the start of the new millennium. Scientific evidence shows that meditation can provide benefits for a wide range of health conditions. The evidence from countless research studies indicates that daily meditation practice helps improve various biological, neurological, psychological, and social functions.

The health science literature shows that the practice of daily meditation is a dependable and effective resource for maintaining good psychological, emotional, moral, and social health. Health researchers demonstrate that meditation enhances people's health and human development. It promotes harmony between the mind, body, and spirit, benefiting all aspects of health. Studies indicate that meditation lowers the risk of high blood pressure, heart disease, strokes, and inflammatory disorders, while boosting the immune system's vitality. Meditation is also shown to improve neurocognitive functions, foster psychological stability, cultivate emotional balance, prevent substance abuse and addictive behaviors, improve sleep patterns, and encourage healthier diet habits.[57]

Neuroscience emphasizes that meditation helps improve emotional maturity and emotional intelligence. Researchers have shown that people who practice daily meditation—compared to those who do not—score higher on psychological mindfulness, intrapersonal and interpersonal perceptiveness, self-awareness, self-control, self-regulatory behaviors, holistic wellness, and good mental health.[58]

Over the past few decades, neuroscientists have extensively studied the effects of meditation on the human brain. They demonstrate that brain mechanisms resulting from meditation are beneficial for developing cognitive abilities necessary for practical wisdom, which is essential for living effectively in a rapidly changing world. Meditation enhances emotional regulation and cognitive clarity, helping to improve daily relationships. Many view it as an important resource not only for enhancing people's health but also for fostering a healthier humanity.

Neuroscientists have discovered that meditation can enable the

---

[57] Luders E, Clark K, Narr KL, Toga AW. Enhanced Brain Connectivity in Long-term Meditation Practitioners. Neuroscience, August 2011

[58] NIH Website. MEDITATION AND MINDFULNESS: WHAT YOU NEED TO KNOW

nervous system and brain to be transformed and reorganized, leading to the creation of new neural pathways. They demonstrate that meditation can positively influence the brain's neuroplasticity, helping it to evolve and improve higher mental abilities.[59]

Neuroscience research shows that daily meditation can rewire the brain to respond effectively to stressful situations. Researchers found that meditation activates the "relaxation response" and turns off the usual "fight or flight" response. The evidence indicates that meditation helps promote the parasympathetic nervous system.

Neuroscience highlights the limitless potential of the human brain that is waiting to be unlocked. The neuroplasticity induced by meditation develops and creates pathways that enhance communication between the left and right brain hemispheres to a degree unlike before. Usually, one hemisphere is more developed than the other, causing imbalances in thinking, perceptions, and experiences of reality. Meditation has been found to enable both hemispheres of the brain to work together in harmony and unlock the untapped, limitless potentials of the human mind.

Neuroimaging and neurochemistry have made it possible to measure changes in brain mechanisms and chemicals caused by meditation. Researchers have shown that meditation reduces brain arousal during highly stressful situations.[60] Practicing meditation daily helps the brain naturally produce vital chemicals that pharmaceutical companies typically synthesize in labs. The chemicals serotonin, dopamine, adrenaline, and cortisol are among the most well-known measurable changes in brain chemistry resulting from meditation. Systematic reviews and meta-analyses of empirical research on meditation have ranked it alongside antidepressants.

---

[59] Fox KCR, Nijebeor S, et.al. Is Meditation Associated With Altered Brain Structure? A Systematic Review and Meta-Analysis of Morphometric Neuroimaging in Meditation Practitioners. Neuroscience & Biobehavioral Reviews 2014

[60] Lagopoulos et al. Increased Theta and Alpha EEG Activity During Nondirective Meditation. The Journal of Alternative and Complementary Medicine (Vol 15), 2009

Furthermore, meditation is shown to positively affect the amygdala, a part of the brain linked to anxiety, stress, and emotional regulation. Neuroscience states that meditation can significantly increase the grey matter in the posterior cingulate cortex, which boosts concentration and memory. As a result, practicing meditation daily helps strengthen cognitive control, improving mood and reducing stress.

The documented research in neuroscience demonstrates the positive effects of meditation on brain waves. These waves range from very fast to very slow. Each of the five types of brain waves is linked to different effects on a person. Researchers have found that alpha and theta brain waves usually dominate during meditation.[61] These waves are known to improve mental clarity, emotional stability, and behavioral responses. People who meditate daily experience these benefits through better memory, less anxiety, greater adaptability, and enhanced complex skills like creativity.

Neuroscience indicates that meditation not only benefits brain waves but also uncovers a link between brain waves and human consciousness. Researchers have discovered that individuals who operate with alpha and theta brainwaves demonstrate higher levels of consciousness.[62] This is evident in greater self-awareness, social awareness, reciprocity, empathy, compassion, and tolerance. They show improved ethical thinking and responsibility. Overall, they maintain a positive bio-energy field that positively influences others they interact with. All of this suggests that meditation can help unlock the innate human potential and skills that are typically dormant.

Today, scientists are discovering that there is a unified intelligent consciousness that pervades the entire universe.[63] Some believe it is an omnipresent and omniscient force existing in every atom and particle of life,

---

[62] Katyal S. & Goldin P. Alpha and theta oscillations are inversely related to progressive levels of meditation depth. Neuroci Conscious. (Vol 2021 Issue 1), Nov 2021
[63] Dainton B, Stream of Consciousness: Unity and Continuity in Conscious Experience. (2ndEd). Routledge, 2005.

including humans. They suggest that the phenomenon of 'All-in-all,' divine spirit, or 'universal consciousness' is no longer just a philosophical idea or an unproven theory on the fringes of metaphysics. Modern science is beginning to show that the phenomenon of a quantum mind truly exists and can access the universe's quantum field. Some have found that meditation helps develop a quantum mind capable of connecting with the quantum universe.

All of the above emphasize meditation as a powerful tool for enhancing spiritual health, with positive effects on other areas of health. In today's world, neuroscience, medical science, psychology, and health sciences have widely recognized meditation as a valuable practice. Health sciences strongly support meditation as a solution for the epidemic of restless minds today and as a remedy for its negative health impacts. Numerous research studies have made meditation a compelling and practical addition to conventional healthcare.

The modern health system recognizes meditation as a mainstream method to promote and enhance holistic health. As both a preventive and curative treatment, the use of meditation is grounded in scientific evidence — without any religious associations. As a daily health resource, meditation deepens self-awareness. It helps people stay connected to their core reality and the inner workings of the mind, allowing them to be true to their authentic selves in life. Meditation can benefit people from all backgrounds, pursuits, and life situations. Today, health providers and professionals recommend making meditation a part of daily routines to support good health.

The term "meditation" encompasses a wide range of practices used by individuals with an inner-centered approach to life. It may include the practice of the Rosary among Catholics, Subah among Muslims, or Shlokas among Hindus. In scientific literature, "meditation" often refers to the traditional form known as mindfulness meditation, which is more common in Eastern traditions. This involves bringing complete attention to the present experience moment by moment. It is non-discursive and differs from the discursive forms of meditation, often called contemplation, which are more common in Western traditions. Both discursive and non-discursive meditation practices have been used for centuries.

The more common practice of meditation for building spiritual health is non-discursive, following the traditional methods of Eastern traditions. It involves sitting in a still posture for approximately 20 to 30 minutes, or for a longer preferred duration—some choose to meditate daily for 45 minutes to an hour per session. It also requires focusing on breathing with sustained concentration while observing the flow of thoughts without reacting to them. This process turns the 'observer' in meditation into the 'observed.' The crucial aspect is maintaining deep concentration on the breath or another object, while gently watching the flow of thoughts without engaging with them, and minimizing focus on the breathing or object of concentration.

Experts suggest practicing meditation more than once daily. However, it is not meant to add another item to a busy schedule. Instead, it aims to help individuals slow down, become more attentive, and feel less overwhelmed by life's constant rush. In monastic traditions of both East and West, meditation was practiced before breakfast, lunch, and dinner. It is believed that practicing at 4- to 5-hour intervals benefits the body's natural balance.

Today, people realize that growing spiritual health not only benefits the individual but also helps humanity and the planet. More individuals believe that their own survival is linked to the survival of all. They are discovering that their daily meditation practice offers profound therapeutic benefits for all of humanity. People commit to daily meditation not only as a way to improve personal health but also as a way to enhance the health of society and positively impact humanity and the planet.

We will make a significantly purposeful investment in learning and practicing meditation daily. It is an investment that benefits all of humanity. Consistent meditation practice can yield valuable rewards that everyone can share. Meditation should be seen as a vital resource for the entire human race to be present and live in the moment.

Journaling

Journal writing is an ancient practice that dates back to at least the second century. Since ancient times, personal journals have been used to express private thoughts and feelings. Usually, it was done to acknowledge one's blessings and confess shortcomings.

Since around the 18th century, the practice of keeping a journal has become popular. It was widely used by people from all walks of life, including royalty, statesmen, politicians, national leaders, social revolutionaries, intellectuals, authors, and actors. The purpose of journal writing was initially to record life's happenings and events. However, in the process, the writer also managed to create a meaningful narrative of life as it unfolded and develop a deeper self-understanding.

Today, health experts say that after talk therapy, journal writing is the most effective way for emotional release. Health professionals find that the practice helps patients improve in thinking and feeling, develop better social skills, and maintain better physical and mental health.

Among the steps toward a "healthy me," journal writing is the most often overlooked. Health researchers show that journal writing offers many essential health benefits. Over the past twenty years, researchers have found that journaling helps people build resilience, manage emotions, lower stress, improve moods, grow more optimistic, boost self-confidence, overcome inhibitions, reduce symptoms of depression, and more.[64]

Journal writing can be an affordable and convenient form of healthcare. In health literature, it is seen as an effective tool for both prevention and treatment. It enhances cognitive integration, helping people better perceive and understand the sabotaging forces within themselves. Researchers have documented evidence showing that journal writing is suitable for all age groups,

---

[64] Ruini C and Mortara C, <u>Writing Technique Across Psychotherapies – From Traditional Expressive Writing to New Positive Psychology interventions: A Narrative Review</u>. J Contemp Psychother (52) 2022

demographics, and life situations.[65]

Furthermore, researchers have shown that journal writing helps both patients and healthy individuals foster positive self-regard, alter unhealthy habits, and enhance lifestyles. Regular journaling enables people to improve in self-care behaviors, reduce their reliance on prescription medications, and make fewer visits to the doctor.[66]

Health sciences view journaling as a crucial tool in the ongoing healing of the mind, body, and spirit.[67] Health experts highlight that the psycho-emotional processes involved in journal writing provide therapeutic benefits. Health scientists see journal writing as an emotion-focused self-regulation method with many positive effects on mental and physical health. The experiences of everyday people show that practicing journal writing greatly helps reduce the impact of internal stressors.

Neuroscience suggests that the healing process during journal work involves activating the full capacity of the brain.[68] Researchers discovered that regular journal writing gradually calms the amygdala. The amygdala mediates emotional learning and regulates emotional behavior. They believe this results from a better understanding of daily emotional experiences. They assert that when emotions are understood, they are experienced with less intensity than when they are not.

Neuroscience researchers also observed greater activation in the striatum during journaling.[69] Along with the prefrontal cortex, the striatum supports the cognitive control of memory retrieval. They point out

---

[65] Smyth JM, Johnson J, et.al. Journaling in the Improvement of Mental Distress and Well-being in General Medical Patients with Elevated Anxiety Symptoms: A Prelominary Randomized Controlled Trail. JMIR Mental Health, October 2018
[66] Gortner EM, Rude SS, Pennebaker JW, Benefits of Expressive Writing in Lowering Rumination and Depressive Symptoms. Behavior Therapy (37), 2006
[67] McAdams DP, Bauer JJ, et.al. Continuity and Change in the Life Story: A Longitudinal Study of Autobiographical Memories in Emerging Adulthood. Journal of Personality, (74) 2006.
[68] Rajmohan V, Mohandas E. The Limbic System. Indian J Psychiatry. Vol. 49 Issue 2; 2007
[69] DeMenichi BC, et.al. Effects of Expressive Writing on Neural Processing During Learning. Front. Hum. Neurosci., November 2019

that journal writing affects the brain network and function. They maintain that the information in journaling is more easily transferred from short-term to long-term memory. It is as if, during journaling, the journal writer signals to the brain that what is written is more important.

Modern psychology suggests that journaling accesses the left brain, which is analytical and rational. When the left brain is engaged, the right brain is free to create, intuit, and feel. It highlights that the therapeutic benefits of journaling come from transferring information from long-term memory to working (short-term) memory, which enhances dispositional awareness and positively influences daily thoughts, perceptions, and interpretations of events and experiences in one's life.

Research conducted in mental health has shown that journal writing offers benefits to patients diagnosed with major depressive disorder and anxiety disorder.[70] The researchers highlight that journal writing helps individuals reconcile with their past, improve self-acceptance, and reduce mental distress. They also found that people experienced improvements in emotional intelligence and enhanced interpersonal skills.

Researchers in medical science have shown that journal writing provides clinical benefits for patients with blood pressure issues, cardiovascular diseases, autoimmune and inflammatory conditions, fibromyalgia, irritable bowel syndrome, HIV, and AIDS. They have also linked journaling to consistent improvements in the well-being of cancer patients.

Health experts highlight that writing about everyday experiences and the chatter of the "monkey mind" helps the journal writer gain inner stability, feel more balanced, and stay grounded. Research shows that the simple habit of recording life's challenges, joyful moments, and everything in between can

---

[70] Smyth JM, et.al. Online Positive Affect Journaling in the Improvement of Mental Distress and Well-Being in General Medical Patients With Elevated Anxiety Symptoms: A Preliminary Randomized Controlled Trial, JMIR Publication (Vol. 5); 2018

eliminate subtle factors that negatively impact health.

Overall, journal writing benefits people's spiritual, physical, psychological, emotional, mental, and social health. It fosters better human psychology, promoting positive growth, self-development, and well-being. Health sciences recognize journal writing as an important healthcare practice. Health experts assert that although it does not provide a formal diagnosis, journaling offers the healing power of addressing psycho-spiritual, psycho-physical, psycho-emotional, and psycho-social issues that adversely affect health and quality of life.

In literature, the testimonies of many journal keepers show that journaling enhances dispositional awareness. It creates a synergistic interaction between evolving human consciousness and real-life events and experiences. Journaling has served as a valuable resource for self-evolution. The practice helps the writer stay true to the real self and grow in the higher self. Essentially, journal work builds the holistic person and harnesses the innate potential of spiritual human nature, influencing the way people think, behave, and live.

In health literature, it is emphasized that the purpose of journal writing should be solely for its own sake and not driven by the desire to leave any legacy. The healing in journal writing comes from being honest with oneself – journal work mainly acts as a mirror to reflect who you are. Journal writing benefits the writer by allowing them to record their deepest thoughts, feelings, experiences, and life events in a way that is based solely on "as-is" reality, truth, and fact. Regular journal writers report spending about 20 minutes a day on journal writing, although many days may go beyond that.

To sum up:

The journal serves as a logbook of the journey toward a "healthy me." It provides a non-judgmental record of the ups and downs of everyday life events and experiences. It involves writing about life's happenings, interactions, thoughts, feelings, and almost every matter that one might usually avoid talking about or sharing with others.

As a spiritual health practice, journaling helps us delve into the work that is essential for being free from the inside out. The journal process serves as a training ground for tuning into the affected mental processes, understanding the core inner reality, and staying true to the true self. It provides new insights and clarity about one's personhood and the ability to distinguish the "real self" from the "actual self" or "pseudo self," ultimately supporting self-evolution toward becoming a holistic person in life and developing the higher-order personhood or the "higher self."

The art of journal writing involves backward reviewing, moving from the present moment back in time to recall events, interactions, and accompanying thoughts and feelings. It provides a fact-based description of information, affirming the "as-is" reality of real-time life. It is not intended to be a commentary, interpretation, or a "post-mortem" of the bare facts. Instead, it objectively explores one's deepest thoughts, feelings, and associated behaviors.

By recording real-life experiences in writing, journaling becomes a dedicated time to tune into the daily chatter of the "monkey mind". The written expression of hidden thoughts and feelings about real-life experiences helps connect the mind's chatter, such as ruminative thinking and worrying, to perceptions, choices, decisions, and behaviors in everyday life.

Journal work provides a safe space to confront issues we often avoid and deny, rather than hiding them from ourselves. It is a place to reflect on one's deepest feelings and thoughts. During journal writing, one feels comfortable exploring the deeper parts of the mind and heart. However, this exploration of thoughts, feelings, and experiences occurs without getting stuck in them. The process of writing becomes a mirror for self-reflection and gaining insights into how the actual self overrides the real self in daily life.

No one can avoid the messy and painful experiences we all face in life. We tend to carry these experiences with us every day, and they can weigh us down. However, we cannot be alert as life happens or be "fully alive" in the present moment if we are stuck in the past. Pain, anger, frustration, despair, fear, and all negativity need to be released, much like a pressure cooker's release valve. Mental and emotional pressures are like steam that builds up inside a pressure cooker. Journaling acts as the release valve, allowing those pressures to escape.

Writing about upsetting, challenging, or traumatic events in a journal lets us release negative feelings and emotions. We eliminate the unhelpful stuff that weighs us down. At the same time, journal work also helps us capture many positive mental and emotional benefits from our good experiences. We uncover the positive traits and qualities within us. We strengthen our inherent potential as spiritual human beings.

The practice of sitting quietly and writing with a focused mind creates an "inner space" to understand, perceive, and discern deeply rooted and complex psycho-emotional elements. We unravel subconscious and unconscious destructive thought patterns, feelings, and behaviors. Journal work establishes the "inner environment" needed for the processes of "becoming" and "renewing" in life.

The scribbled words serve as a psychological blueprint of the person's evolving self. Journal work helps individuals develop a sense of self rooted in ongoing self-discovery. Journaling increases awareness of the true self versus the actual self and reinforces our ability to distinguish between the two in daily life. The journal writer is confident in a self-identity that emerges from constant self-evolution and creates a life orientation and goals aligned with the true self, objective truths, and higher purposes.

Experts assert that journal writing stimulates new insights and strengthens willpower to break nesting habits and challenge psycho-emotional comfort zones. The health literature highlights that the practice reprograms the subconscious mind, allowing it to access higher cognitive functions like insight and intuition. This process helps us unlock practical wisdom that has been dormant. Ultimately, our deepest values and higher goals that we truly cherish become more prominent in our consciousness.

As a practice for spiritual health, journal work is the support we give ourselves to better perceive, understand, and interpret simple and everyday life matters and to see how they influence who we truly are. Journal work helps us learn how to be human daily in the world. All of us carry the potential for goodness, the best, and the noblest. Writing in a journal helps build a way of life that aligns with these qualities.

The French novelist Marcel Proust said, "The voyage of discovery lies not in seeking new vistas but in having new eyes." Journal writing gives us "new eyes" to navigate through all the circumstances of life. The practice strengthens the ability to live in the here-and-now present moment. We grow in the art of not fighting what life offers us but becoming skillful in navigating our way through all life's hurdles with deeper insights, intuitive abilities, and inherent wisdom – we live with the "soul intelligence" of a higher self.

Inspirational Reading

Modern science is uncovering many health benefits of reading. In scientific literature, some of the most notable advantages include improved memory and concentration. It is also claimed that people who read daily develop stronger thinking and analytical skills. Additionally, the habit of reading helps people cultivate calmness, reduce stress, empathize more, enhance intrapersonal and interpersonal skills, and ease psycho-emotional symptoms. Most importantly, those who read every day are known to live longer.

The habit of reading inspirational books and literature benefits people by encouraging self-reflection, self-understanding, and self-evolution. The reader gains insight into the inner workings of the mind and develops perspectives on their way of being and living. It helps to confront the core inner reality and recognize the true self as distinct from the actual self or pseudo-self. This is why some healthcare practitioners now even recommend reading as part of treatment.

Since the dawn of civilization, the practice of inspirational reading has been used to develop the human mind and strengthen the human psyche. Inspirational reading helped people cultivate higher ideals and discover a greater purpose in life. People turned to the wise and learned works written by scholars to create a map of human nature that promoted high ideals and meaningful purposes in life, rather than succumbing to primitive or uncivilized tendencies.

Today, we often find ourselves trapped in cycles of repetitive, negative thoughts that carry a dark emotional weight. These daily patterns of thinking and feeling diminish our true selves. We struggle—if not find it impossible—to shift our minds toward higher ideals and purposes. We do not prioritize building a more meaningful life filled with graciousness, soulfulness, and virtue. The importance of inspirational reading is now greater than ever in human history.

Before the electronic era, daily reading was almost a universal ritual for those who could read and write. In many socio-economically underdeveloped societies, even those who could not read benefited from inspirational books. There were regular community programs where such books were read aloud. Today, however, people are so absorbed in social media and the internet that few take the time to read books. Additionally, in our digital world, the fast pace of life makes it harder to develop the habit of reflective reading. Reading habits become more difficult as people's attention spans weaken, making it hard to focus on anything for more than a few minutes; some experts say it's just seconds.

Furthermore, the habit of reading faces many competing influences that stimulate the mind in today's world. In our digital age, numerous technological devices and entertainment options compete fiercely for our attention. People find themselves addicted to the stimulation from the entertainment industry, salacious material on the internet, fake news media, the frantic energy of social media, and similar distractions. Electronic media continuously deposit a pile of mental debris on everyone in society. We dwell in a "negative mind" caused by disinformation, excessive passions, feelings of hostility and hate, and other negative influences.

In our world, we are immersed in a cultural environment where there is no escape from mental stimulants of all kinds. The obsession with social media apps pulls us into each other's negative mental states. On the internet, the human mind engages in mental garbage collection every day from one another. We are constantly feeding our minds junk without even realizing it. Additionally, people tend to fall into negative habits of the mind, such as worrying, judging, blaming, and similar behaviors. Without the intention and motivation to free ourselves from within, we will continue to engage in mental clutter every single day without realizing it is happening.

Ordinary people often feel that the "negative mind" outweighs the "positive mind." However, they are unaware of the clutter in their minds and the chaos it causes. For most in society, it seems almost impossible to "let go" and "let be" because they cannot access the "positive mind." They are limited in their views and perspectives on how to handle destructive mental tendencies better and live healthily. They are not truly free from within. They experience a human spirit that weakens the personal "freedoms" they desire. More often than acknowledged, we harm ourselves daily by engaging in destructive thinking patterns that lead to harmful behaviors with consequences for us and others.

All the problems in personal life and modern society, along with all the evildoing in the postmodern world, show that the "negative mind" weakens the transformative powers of the human mind. There is always a need to eliminate the "negative mind." But there is no magic pill to accomplish this. We often feel helpless against a "negative mind" that refuses to go away. No matter how hard we try, it persists. Purging the 'negative mind' is always a challenge, but it is not impossible. It occurs when we interrupt the flow of negative thoughts with positivity, enthusiasm, and higher ideals.

Another way to put it, the human mind and spirit require nutrients just like the physical body does. Today, we nourish the mind and spirit no differently than we nourish the body. We consume "junk food" for the body, mind, and spirit. The world we live in tends to be more indulgent. The enticing stimulation of our sensory world is irresistible, leading people to indulge in hedonic whims and fancies constantly.

Since ancient times, inspirational reading has been a practice used to nourish the mind with positive aspirations and higher ideals to reduce the effects of negative thoughts. Inspirational books act as doors that can unlock our thinking and imagination, elevating our self-experience to a new level. They introduce us to the deeper reality of the human person that lies dormant within us. Inspirational reading is an important spiritual health practice because it guides us along a path of progress in life. It helps us harness our potential to create a more radiant life.

Everyone recognizes the powerful influence of a trusted friend's voice, which offers candid advice, supports with good counsel, corrects, encourages, and guides us away from mistakes. The voice is never harsh, the advice is always selfless, and the words are never timid or deceptive. Its sole purpose is to help us clarify our thoughts, uplift our spirits, and enhance our well-being. The voice provides abundant healing without the person realizing it is being done to us.

The same happens when we read inspirational books – we form bonds with mentors who offer us self-renewal, inner healing, growth, and inner freedom. They create a "positive mind," helping us live intentionally and purposefully. These mentors can be from the distant past or present, accessed only through their writings. They teach us through books, speeches, and recorded discourses. This is precisely how reading inspirational books functions as a practice of spiritual health. Inspirational books positively energize and revitalize the human spirit.

It's essential to recognize that in a world plagued by overwhelming moral, political, and ideological pressures, not everything we consume is genuinely inspiring. Nowadays, we're surrounded by a multitude of self-proclaimed experts, influencers, consultants, and the like, who often appear more focused on peddling ideologies than providing genuine inspiration. Some of these individuals deliberately spread mental poison, further eroding our mental well-being and exacerbating the "negative mind." True inspiration, on the other hand, is a life-changing experience that happens when we tap into our "higher self" and strive to become a better version of ourselves.

The practice of reading inspirational books has been used for centuries as a form of daily therapy. In a sense, inspirational reading is a kind of therapy session. Like meditation and journaling, it gains healing benefits because a quieted mind helps focus on the present moment. It increases awareness of the inner processes of the mind. It helps us recognize our inner-core reality and how it affects us. We clear the way for the real self to take on an active role in guiding how we behave and live in the world.

The habit of reading encourages us to spend time alone in a positively beneficial way. Inspirational books help us to create images in our mind of the better version of ourselves we can become. While reading, there is a feeling of comfort, but often, there is also a sense of confrontation with ourselves. We begin to see what our "as-is" self-reality truly is. It promotes self-evolution and helps a person develop their sense of personhood. We come face-to-face with the "as-is" real me. There is an awakening to not deny the true self and to recognize that it may differ from the actual self or pseudo self.

Inspirational reading helps us connect more with the better version of ourselves—the person we have the potential to become that lies dormant within us. We commit to the "renewal" and "becoming" we need in the present through the inspiration of higher-order thinking, values, attitudes, principles, and behaviors. We grow in the spirit of forgiveness, compassion, temperance, and altruism. We find hope when despair looms over us, allowing us to move forward in life. We strive to be who we can be and genuinely are, despite the inescapable soul-killing cultural influences, sensational distractions, and the nonstop streaming of electronic media.

The practice of reading inspirational material can be life-changing in many ways. When life's pressures drain our "renewal energy," inspirational reading provides the remedy. It helps restore calm, balance, and objectivity in everyday life. We gain deeper insights into life's true meaning, pursue higher purposes, and eliminate negative thought patterns. We learn to build and sustain a healing relationship with ourselves and others. Essentially, daily reading of inspirational books brings clarity and motivation to develop a healthy, well-rounded human being. It benefits spiritual health by helping us piece together fragmented personhood and grow into a "whole" self.

In health science literature, inspirational reading is seen as an effective way to explore the inner workings of the mind and enhance the mental skills needed to navigate life. People who engage in inspirational reading find it a powerful tool to heal and mend their fractured sense of self. It offers them creative ideas for becoming a better person and promotes thinking and experiences of self-evolution. One transcends the ordinary and experiences a higher form of personhood. The limited self-identity shaped by biology and culture is renewed with the discovery of the "higher self."

Inspirational reading is seen as a form of "spiritual exercise" in both science and religion. For centuries, the benefits of inspirational reading were believed to come from personal experiences alone, but now science helps us understand its importance even more. A growing body of research shows that reading actually changes the human brain and refreshes the mind.[71] Using MRI scans, researchers have confirmed that reading activates a complex network of circuits and signals in the brain. As the habit of reading becomes regular, these networks also become stronger and more sophisticated.

Today, researchers show that during reading, there is an increase in the brain connectivity of the somatosensory cortex, the part of the brain that responds to sensations and emotions. This allows people to understand feelings

---

[71] Kidd DC and Castano E, <u>Reading Literary Fiction Improves Theory of Mind</u>. Science, October 2013.

better, improve empathy, and create space for themselves and others to be and grow. People develop stronger self-acceptance and accept others for who they are and where they are in life.

Researchers also demonstrated that inspirational reading lowers blood pressure and heart rate, reduces psychological distress, and helps manage high levels of stress in people.[72] When individuals feel isolated and estranged from everyone—and show early signs of clinical depression—the habit of inspirational reading has proven to be an effective strategy for managing pain or depression symptoms.

What modern science is revealing is that inspirational reading is a practice that supports the development of spiritual health in daily life. The complex network of brain circuits formed by inspirational reading likely supports the function of the "spiritual brain." As mentioned earlier, the "spiritual brain" is the "neurobiological home" of spiritual health.

Health experts say that inspirational reading material is unlimited and not just limited to religious scriptures and devotional books. While reading religious scriptures and devotional books has its benefits, it can also restrict the mind. The negative view of "people of the book" often refers to individuals whose thinking is limited by narrow worldviews and illogical, irrational ideas.

We live in a time where religious scriptures are used to justify what is simply wrong and evil about human life in the postmodern world. Evidence from life shows us that religious scriptures and books often pressure people to create worldviews that limit their thinking patterns in daily life. Much of what relates to human reality is redacted in the conscious mind. The dogmatic thinking patterns developed by obsessions with scriptural texts block what is factual about one's everyday human life and existence.

Today, some theologians agree that religious scriptures do not have the

---

[72] Lewis, D. Physical and mental health benefits of reading books. Galaxy Stress Research, Mindlab International University of Sussex; 2009

final say and move away from the idea that truth must come solely from theological sources and ideals. People turn to resources beyond scriptures and religious books to gain deeper self-awareness, find life's deeper meaning, and broaden their perspectives. In reality, the "truth" we seek is uncovered when we are prepared for it. As the saying of the Buddha often quoted to seekers of truth, "When the student is ready, the teacher will arrive."

Furthermore, to gain the health benefits of inspirational reading, experts recommend making it a daily spiritual practice for about 20 to 30 minutes. The dedication to reading inspirational books is similar to the commitment to practicing meditation, journaling, or maintaining good physical health through diet, exercise, leisure, and sleep.

Experts highlight that inspiring reading not only fulfills immediate needs and goals, like those achieved during a therapy session, but also offers long-term benefits, such as those from seeking therapy. It provides a temporary escape from an overwhelming mental and emotional world while effectively reshaping thinking patterns. As British philosopher Sir Roger Scruton said, "Consolation from imaginary things is not an imaginary consolation."

To sum up:

The practice of inspirational reading is the sanctuary where all our inner truths emerge in life. It strengthens the muscle of truth in the human mind. It reveals the many dangers that threaten the path of self-deception. It unsettles our deceitful self-complacency.

Through this practice, we increase our understanding of our metaphysical human nature. We learn to think more clearly and realistically when making choices and decisions in life. The recklessness and imbalance of our self-delusions give way to the objective truth and staying true to the real self. Inspirational reading opens the "third eye" for the "higher self" to develop in one's personhood. There is always a richer personality style and functioning brought to life by one's "higher self".

The "higher self" is also called the "metaphysical self" or

"transcendental self." It represents an individual's embodiment and expression of "soulful intelligence." In modern psychology, the "higher self" is seen as a uniquely human ability that can be cultivated within a person's personality. In theology—especially mystical theology—it symbolizes the innate human-divine connection.

The Sanskrit term "citta" (truth-of-the-heart) refers to the higher self as the source of the broad range of cognitive and emotional states within a person. "Citta" signifies the ability to detach from the "egotistical self," which is often the "pseudo-self," and to express the higher self. The "soul" – the metaphysical essence of human nature – is the primary expression of the true and "whole" human reality within us.

In human consciousness literature, the "third eye" refers to the gateway to the inner realms and higher states of awareness. In religion, it is a symbol of enlightenment. The discovery of the pineal gland by modern science—the last endocrine gland to be identified, located deep in the center of the brain, and its connection to light through the circadian rhythm and melatonin secretion—has led some to believe there is a neurobiological basis for the "third eye." They describe the "third eye" as "the spirit molecule" or "the seat of the soul".

Basically, the "third eye" represents the higher intelligence inherent in humans. It is experienced through intuition, psycho-emotional clarity, higher sense perception, unified consciousness, and the ability to harmonize the mind-body-spirit-environment dimensions at all times. Everyone can develop and tap into this higher intelligence. Regular practice of inspirational reading, meditation, and journaling is how we open the "third eye" and cultivate this higher intelligence for everyday life.

The "third eye" is the link to our higher self. Practicing inspirational reading, by opening the "third eye," helps the true self and higher self when blocked by the illusions of the pseudo-self. Inspirational reading taps into the natural wisdom in people, allowing the true self and higher self to live more effectively. They realize their innate abilities for deeper awareness, insight, intuition, and practical wisdom to achieve holism.

Since ancient times, all cultures and societies have practiced reading inspirational books aimed at opening the "third eye" and awakening the "higher self." Through this practice, people have accessed guidance and training from mentors who inspire the shimmering life, helping to develop the "higher self." The teachings and writings of these mentors act like prescriptions for cultivating the "higher self" as a vital resource for spiritual health.

The world we live in is changing, and books can serve as gateways to the "higher self." The inspiration and wisdom gained through inspirational reading open the "third eye" and nurture the "higher self." Apparently, in our times, this human phenomenon is a forgotten resource within people's personhood. We are missing out on the guidance we need daily to discover the "new way" of being 'fully human and fully alive.' Today, we are in desperate need of individuals who can model for us the higher self and a shimmering life.

Inspirational reading acts as a catalyst for discovering the true self and the higher self. It can shape a self-identity that is not limited by biology, psychology, or culture. Typically, a person's self-identity can come from the pseudo-self, real self, or higher self. The pseudo-self represents self-preservation, the real self signifies self-liberation, and the higher self indicates self-actualization. While the pseudo-self naturally experiences doubt about self-identity and the real self aims to clarify it, the higher self's role is to manifest a new reality of self-identity.

The journey to a "healthy me" is surprisingly long, spanning the distance from the pseudo-self to the real self and then to one's higher self. One's ability to set each aspect of one's personhood and life in proper perspective is almost always linked to the practice of inspirational reading.

The goal of inspirational reading is not to create more mental clutter or overload our already crowded minds, but to help the mind stay in the "healthy lane." The "higher self" is always the best resource to prevent us from straying from the "healthy lane." Inspirational reading guides us to live freely from within by helping us keep the "third eye" open and develop the "higher self."

We must view these four evidence-based practices for growing spiritual health as essential to one's personhood and sense of self, much like hydrogen fuel is to the sun or nuclear fusion is to solar energy. These practices are almost essential for building a sense of "wholeness" in personhood and holistic selfhood. The holistic person and way of life are the best expressions of one's spiritual human nature and spiritual health. Spiritual health is the lifelong process of self-evolution that individuals undergo to become the "whole" human being designed by nature.

One's holistic health and holistic living are fundamentally governed by the "spiritual law" of nature, rather than any material or man-made law. This law is embedded in the spiritual principles of ethical living and simple living, which are not optional choices but rather necessities of the natural world. These spiritual principles consistently enhance spiritual technologies to foster spiritual health.

A person's spiritual health is best judged by how they live each day, rather than merely fulfilling religious duties and obligations. It is evaluated by the inner being, not by outward appearances, behaviors, or standards of a religion or "spiritual system." The inner qualities of honesty, honor, integrity, goodness, compassion, tolerance, and altruism—those human traits that reflect a vibrant and noble life—are what shape people's opinions of someone's spiritual health.

People who experience spiritual health show that the "good life" involves embracing the human essence—our metaphysical nature—and that what matters most in life is bringing this human essence to the forefront of daily living. Adopting a life focused on ethics and simplicity naturally follows when the human essence is prioritized. An individual developing in higher levels of consciousness—tangibly expressed through the "higher self"—shapes this life approach. Ethical behaviors and simple lifestyles always interact in a harmonious, synergistic way in the experience of a person's spiritual health.

Ethical thinking and simple living stem from the life-animating principle of one's "real self" and the "soul intelligence" of the "higher self." The "real self" and "higher self" foster a way of life characterized by higher-order thinking, comprehensive life perspectives, and a balance of responsibility, all while fostering a deeper connection within the web of life. The humaneness shown by a holistic human is unmatched. The implications of this lifestyle are discussed in relation to increasing spiritual health in everyday life.

Ethical Living

The spiritual human nature that sets us apart from other animals is mainly demonstrated through our ethical abilities. Moral human nature greatly enhances and emphasizes the spiritual aspect of human nature. While animals are guided solely by instincts, humans rely on rational thinking, pursue objective truth, intuition, and practical wisdom to direct and shape their lives.

As humans, we are uniquely endowed with the innate potential to overcome primitive tendencies, savage impulses, and unrefined behaviors. It is always a choice made every single day to elevate to the spiritual human nature. All that is required to reflect what it means to be truly human is primarily about living deliberately and intentionally.

Humans can engage in a pre-reflective mental process and become phenomenally aware of reasoning, choices, decisions, and behaviors. The advanced cognitive functions of the human brain allow for moral awareness and practical deliberation, enabling individuals to participate in life with pro-social thoughts, feelings, and behaviors, and to strive beyond set ethical standards.

What best distinguishes the human species in the animal kingdom is essentially our inherent spiritual and moral nature. The spiritual and moral aspects of human nature are central to human consciousness. The mental processes of humans and other animals differ in the spiritual and moral functions of human consciousness. These functions allow humans to understand objective truth, strive for higher ideals and purposes, and develop integrity and character.

We express what makes the "spiritual" in us by engaging with our moral human nature through ethical living. The objective truth within an individual's existential moral realm and the right response to moral challenges and responsibilities are determined by the spiritual and moral functions of human consciousness. Humans have an innate potential to develop qualities such as truthfulness, high-mindedness, goodness, kindness, honor, fairness, empathy, compassion, altruism, and ethical living.

The spiritual and moral are inseparable and cannot be seen as two separate spheres. Both are central to a person's core ideals and deepest aspirations. They influence inner motivations, commitments, and truths. The distinct features of human nature develop through the metaphysical human essence and are rooted in the 'real self'. Ethical living reveals both aspects of human nature in a person's life. It weaves together the spiritual and moral, embodying the dynamics of the inner-core reality and the 'real self' in every thought, emotion, action, and behavior.

The innate spiritual human nature acts as a heuristic device that offers lenses for the ethical way of life. The inherent human capacity for pro-social values like equity, tolerance, and altruism is a gift of spiritual human nature. The "spiritual brain" plays a vital role in developing the "moral being" in a person for ethical living. Essentially, all human virtues, such as kindness, generosity, empathy, and compassion, along with all humane values, attitudes, and behaviors, depend on people's spiritual health.

The spiritual and moral must fundamentally be in a synergistic relationship to encompass the "whole" human person for ethical living. The holistic person and holistic way of life are built on this synergy. The synergy between spiritual and moral intricately influences all ethical aspects of human life. The spiritual and moral lay the foundation for good health and the "good life." Health experts emphasize that the spiritual-moral synergistic interaction, through ethical living, is essential to holistic health.[73]

Higher levels of human consciousness integrate the spiritual and moral nature, serving as a pathway to promote ethical views and practices for ethical living. Evolved human consciousness is a resource that emphasizes objective truth and "as-is" reality, enabling individuals to honor truth and reality in their thoughts, feelings, and behaviors in everyday life.

Today, the neuroscience of moral health offers compelling evidence that ethical behavior is not just a prescriptive discipline but is also closely connected to brain mechanisms. Neuroscience reveals that people's moral senses and actions for ethical living have neurobiological roots.[74] This fundamentally challenges traditional views on normative ethics.

In the postmodern world, the rapid growth of cross-disciplinary research, advancements in cognitive neuroscience, and rising public interest in neuroscience findings all highlight and draw attention to real-world issues related to human health. We have gained a better understanding of the human mind and spirit in various life contexts, as well as the role of human consciousness in living ethically.

Understanding the neurological basis of moral thought and behavior, connected with people's spiritual health, touches on ethical living issues that affect human life on personal, societal, and global levels. The neuroscience of moral health can help us better address the serious problem of poor ethical behavior today by focusing on psycho-emotional aspects of morality, rather than relying solely on traditional morality, conventional practices, or legal measures.

Neuroscience shows us that there is a biological basis for human personality and behavior. It highlights the role of neurobiology in decision-

---

[73] Cheng Q, Wen X, et.al. Neural Underpinnings of Morality Judgment and Moral Aesthetic Judgment. Sci Rep (11) 2021
[74] Smallwood J, Turnbull A, et.al. The Neural Correlates of Ongoing Conscious Thought. iScience (24) Cell Press 2021

making, which affects human actions and relationships. It explains that an individual's choices, decisions, and behaviors can be influenced by various factors—from a person's neurophysiology to personal experiences.

Neuroscientists have also shown that there is a clear neural basis for human consciousness, linking it to complex processes involved in existential thought and decision-making related to ethical behavior.[75] In evaluating responsibility for actions, neuroscience argues that people must be conscious, deliberate, and potentially rational agents of their behaviors.

The fragile nature of the human mind always depends on higher levels of human consciousness to overcome and supplement habitual behaviors that cause everyday ethical problems. Ethical thinking and perceptions of ethical actions develop as human consciousness evolves. Arguably, a person's spiritual health supports the neural foundation of a more expansive and better level of human consciousness, enabling us to move beyond narrow ideas and adopt all-encompassing perspectives that foster the "ethical mind" for pro-social values and behaviors in daily life.

Deeper insights into life stem from the evolving human consciousness of an individual. The evidence in health literature emphasizes that people develop their consciousness through efforts to build spiritual health. The deeper intelligence, instincts, intuitions, and practical wisdom inherent to human nature are by-products of increasing spiritual health. When applied in daily life, these by-products shape an ethical way of living.

The brain mechanisms underlying human consciousness enhance cognitive processes to foster a broad perspective on life and diminish narrower, self-centered viewpoints, including self-absorption and self-indulgence. Developing spiritual health helps individuals overcome the limited views created by a self-centered way of life. As a result, sensitivities and awareness are

---

[75] Joyce J, Gillet G and Devere H, Spiritual Consciousness and the Integrative Brain in Health and Conflict. Journal of Yoga, Phys Ther & Rehab in Gavin Publishers (J119) 2017.

heightened to better relate to others.

Spiritual health reaches its peak and manifests most effectively in the evolving human consciousness, positively enhancing all daily relationships and behaviors. A person's spiritual health is never isolated but always part of a larger network of collective interactive experiences.

Cognitive enhancements from expanded human consciousness allow individuals to interact more effectively with others. This happens in all kinds of environments, in ways that might or might not be achieved through hard work, good habits, and sheer dedication to normative ethics.

Spiritual health involves delving into the depths of the inner-core reality to self-evolve and stay true to the authentic self, as well as cultivating the relationship that the authentic self has with the broader world. The spiritual human nature seeks to let one's meaning and purpose in life emerge from the essential human essence – the metaphysical self, the transcendental self, or the soul. The spiritual core – unlike the malevolent core – and the authentic self drive the motivation to change, adjust, and guide a person toward the "other." Essentially, it is from the spiritual inner-core reality and the authentic self that we discover the other-centered meaning and purpose in life.

The sublime expression of a human person is found in their life values, attitudes, desires, motivations, and behaviors directed toward others. Developing spiritual health cultivates a mindset centered on other people, including values and attitudes that prioritize others. People who nurture spiritual health also develop the motivation to participate in life with prosocial behaviors and to detach from self-centeredness. In everyday life, meaningful human connections and positive relationships depend on prosocial sensitivities and actions. Prosocial attitudes and behaviors are essential to what it means to be human.

Humans uniquely need culture as a species. Culture defines our identity, how we live, and the types of relationships we form. Human life quality and health always exist within the context of culture. We depend on culture to shape our worldviews, influence our values and attitudes, and guide our choices and decisions. We develop lifestyles and goals by adopting cultural ideas and standards.

In today's world, the spirit of consumerism, materialism, and individualism deeply and intricately influences human culture. The global culture tends to suppress one's sense of human virtues, decency, character, integrity, and higher ideals and purposes. This cultural spirit hinders dispositional awareness and essential self-awareness, causing ordinary people to flip-flop on their core beliefs, convictions, and worldviews.

The global culture emphasizes possession-oriented success and a hedonic life orientation. It has fostered a mindset focused on a self-centered way of living. It has convinced almost everyone that the sole purpose of human life is to "make it" at any cost, disregarding anyone or anything else. We live with self-seeking obsessions, drives, and goals that cannot be denied. The consequences of an unethical lifestyle do not matter.

The way to be human involves a tug-of-war with a global culture that cares less about ethical thinking, standards, and living. Evidence from life shows us that the daily drives, ambitions, and habits of ordinary people weaken the importance of self-awareness, self-regulation, and self-control. Many people are unaware of their self-absorption in egocentric behaviors and selfish obsessions. The deeply self-centered way of life is invisible to most today. It hinders the full expression of a person's true human nature. Self-centeredness reflects a flawed personal philosophy, proven by more self-focused behaviors and fewer other-focused ones.

The self-centered way of life stems from a narrow range of ideas. It causes a person to be relentlessly driven by a constant need for self-gratification, regardless of the cost, often ignoring and dismissing the needs, interests, and well-being of others. Today, people's values, priorities, and behavioral and relationship patterns reveal a mindset that seems to originate from an uncontrollable infantile narcissism. It defines self-centered living as the normal way of life in the postmodern world. In a self-centered individual, the pseudo-self becomes the unquestioned reality. The true self is lost amid a host of self-delusions, and the 'higher self' is rarely understood.

The non-self-centered way of life involves valuing oneself and others equally within reciprocal relationships. It reflects a "sense of self" that depends on the "sense of self" of others to feel complete. Existentially, a person's self-worth is diminished if the sense of self from others is lacking. Ethicality relies on both self-value and valuing others.

An individual's spiritual health and ethical living are the points where personal growth and the world meet. Spiritual health and living ethically require a shift in focus toward others, moving away from self-centeredness. Ethical behavior is only evident when we respond to others' needs.

To sum up:

Today, human life poorly reflects human decency, high ideals, righteousness, character, integrity, respect, and honor—values that everyone once strived for. Overall, humanity is failing to demonstrate its true spiritual nature through ethical living.

Today, we tend to downplay and overlook human virtues like forgiveness, compassion, empathy, humility, tolerance, altruism, and nobility. Self-centeredness replaces higher goals and purposes, moderation and austerity, compassion and altruism, and the qualities of higher-order personhood meant to prevent inhumane tendencies, urges, and behaviors.

Spiritual health and ethical living must go hand in hand for a better humanity and a compassionate world. When spiritual health is nurtured, people develop the cognitive, psychological, and emotional balance needed to create a meaningful framework for human life. It provides deeper insight and intuition for clearer psycho-emotional understanding, allowing us to respect human dignity in all relationships and act ethically. We become more motivated to act from a self grounded in a mature and steady moral core characterized by high-mindedness, integrity, and virtue.

The tangible experience of spiritual health is evident in all aspects of wellness, but it relies on building meaningful and healthy relationships. Daily nurturing of one's spiritual health provides opportunities to practice ethical living, positively influencing the "good life" in terms of a well-rounded person, overall health, and a better humanity.

When a person has good spiritual health, it shows in living ethically at all times. Ethicality is the energizing "spiritual force" that drives conscientious individuals who seek peace, harmony, and goodwill in our world. The 'moral self', inspired and motivated by the 'spiritual self,' underpins every good deed performed in the world. It strengthens the commitment, with a conscientious sense of obligation and duty, to care about issues affecting humanity, ecology, and the environment.

People's spiritual health is best reflected through the ability to connect with others and find our shared humanity. When we realize that each of us plays a role in the web of life, we develop better skills for recognizing "otherness" – the value of the 'sense of self' in others – and for overcoming self-centeredness. It is the aptitude for interrelatedness and interconnectivity that positively influences our daily attitudes toward ourselves, others, and the universe as a whole.

The practice of ethical living requires a paradigm shift in how we see ourselves, moving away from cultural constructs. It involves shifting self-value from external standards to an internal one – the moral self. This shift is influenced by self-evolution, which enhances the ability for self-transcendence. Self-transcendence shows a person less motivated by individualism, materialism, and consumerism, and more motivated by a spirit of freedom. It reflects the mature moral self that guides ethical living.

People who are free from the inside out—less affected by spiritual wounds—express the "freedom" of the human spirit and are energized by the power of the spiritual core. Living ethically is always connected to the soulfulness that is brought into life. The person sheds the lenses of cultural phenomena to foster a sense of self aligned with the true self and the higher self.

Ethical living is reflected in high-mindedness, integrity, character, moral strength, and a vibrant life. An ethical person values, honors, and respects the dignity of every human being. By nurturing spiritual health, we can develop the innate human capacities to be truly human in the world and live with a "soul intelligence" to guide us in everyday life.

In today's world, human life can be described as restless, impulsive, reckless, intolerant, impatient, and aggressive. We have become accustomed to denying our true selves and clinging tightly to a false self. We create illusions of the "good life" and indulge in fantasies of happiness and success. We ignore the unpleasant aspects of human life and suppress the existential pain and suffering that are part of human existence. We have no hesitation in harming our own health through various addictions. We refuse to follow the basic principles for a more meaningful human life. Most importantly, in today's society, we neither embrace higher ideals nor uphold fundamental human virtues like integrity and character. All of this reveals that we are desperately struggling with the core aspects of human nature. It underscores the importance of recognizing the potential of spiritual human nature and the urgent need for spiritual health in our world.

The everyday experience of human life shows that there is an overshadowing of the vile, wretched, broken human spirit in all of human existence. Can it be because the "good life" everyone longs for does not include developing spiritual health, which alone can awaken the moral self that supports ethical living?

Simple Living

There is a naive idea that opulence and lavish lifestyles equal the "good life." Nearly everyone associates material prosperity with living the "good life." In today's world, almost everyone pursues success defined by possessions. It's the ultimate life goal for many. The widespread belief is that human fulfillment and happiness depend on material wealth, which is often used to boost one's self-image and self-esteem – of the pseudo-self!

Possession-oriented success and the pursuit of pleasure are effectively eroding human health at its core. We focus on prejudices and biases that prioritize wealth and enjoyment. The thoughts, feelings, and actions of ordinary people are limited by a materialistic mindset and the pursuit of pleasure. The visual appeal of material prosperity, along with the social status and power it confers, hold greater importance and value to a person than their well-being. We are making a serious mistake by allowing ourselves to equate possession-driven success and the pursuit of pleasure with having a "good life".

There has long been a link between materialism and its effects on health. The connection between materialism and health is the most established area of research in the materialism and consumerism literature. At the University of Sussex, a meta-analysis of research on materialism and health shows that the negative relationship between materialism and health was consistent across all types of measures, demographics, locations, and cultures.[76]

Few realize that the main goal of human development is to cultivate mental and emotional skills to meet one's needs in the world. This type of learning always depends on lived experiences. Learning from experiences literally requires experiencing and involves one's human consciousness. Neuroscience emphasizes that learning from lived experiences results from the brain's mechanism of consciousness, which influences cognitive processes to enable better choices and decisions.[77]

Neuroscience has shown that the brain mechanism of consciousness that influences a person's decision-making is different from the one responsible

---

[76] Dittmar H, Bond R, Hurst M and Kasser T, The relationship between materialism and personal well-being: a meta-analysis. Journal of Personality and Social Psychology (Vol 107) 2014
[77] vGaal S, de Lange FP, Cohen MX, The role of consciousness in cognitive control and decision making. Front Hum Neurosci., (vol 6) 2021

for instinctual and emotional impulsiveness.[78] When people embody an acquisitive mindset, success based on possessions, hedonic living, and a pseudo-self, the brain mechanism involved is related to the instinctual and emotional aspects of impulsiveness, not the consciousness that impacts cognitive processes governing choices and decisions.

Furthermore, neuroscience shows that the brain mechanisms of consciousness in people are influenced by the environment. Neuroscientists have demonstrated that a person's personality, along with multifactorial personality and behavioral disorders, results not only from interactions among genes, neurons, and immune and endocrine systems but is also affected by how people respond to natural, social, and cultural environments.[79] Neuroscience highlights that the brain mechanisms behind a person's conscious and unconscious mental states—defining their personality and behavior—are involved in consciousness shaped by the interactive processes between individuals and environmental factors.

Factually, whether our ability to meet human needs is improving or declining depends on influences both inside and outside the brain. The fact that many different environments surround us indicates that we can either develop a consciousness for learning from life experiences or act based on instinctual-emotional sharpness. Today, the human being is heavily immersed in a materialistic and hedonistic environment filled with stimulants. This environment greatly affects brain mechanisms responsible for instinctual-emotional awareness and influences our way of thinking, behaving, and living.

Possession-driven success and the pursuit of pleasure dominate the cultural environment we live in. Individualism, materialism, and hedonism are

---

[78] Bloom FE, Nelson CA, Lazerson A. Brain Mind, and Behavior. 3rd. Worth Publishers 2001.
[79] Huta V, Eudaimonic and Hedonic Orientations: Theoretical Considerations and Research Findings. in Handbook of Eudaimonic Well-Being. Springer, 2016
Adolphs R. The Social Brain: Neural Basis of Social Knowledge. Annual Review of Psychology (vol 60), 2009

the prevailing cultural scripts. This has turned the pseudo-self and compulsive consumption into an epidemic in our society. The daily pursuits of ordinary people are mainly motivated by the material aspects of human nature. The brain mechanisms involved in consciousness are more frequently engaged in instinctual and emotional responses.

Researchers have found that people's materialistic values, attitudes, and pursuits are connected to a hedonic life orientation.[80] Hedonism defines personal well-being and the quality of human life based on pleasure attainment and pain avoidance. The hedonic life orientation focuses on extrinsic values, behaviors, and life goals aimed at building possession-oriented success. The documented evidence shows that extrinsic values are more strongly associated with a hedonic life orientation.

Health researchers have linked hedonic orientation and materialistic values to less interest or motivation in maintaining good health through sustainable methods.[81] They found that people with stronger materialistic values were more likely to engage in behaviors that harm their health. Those who endorse materialistic values more frequently reported physical health issues and experienced more negative emotions, such as depression and anxiety.

Health sciences emphasize that people's intrinsic values support achieving optimal and sustainable health. Researchers have also connected strong intrinsic values in daily life to higher levels of human consciousness.[82] Self-evolution and the growth of human consciousness guide individuals toward humility, simplicity, and reducing habitual consumption. Higher ideals

---

[80] Isham A, Verfeurth C, et.al. The Problematic Role of Materialistic Values in the Pursuit of Sustainable Well-being. Int J Environ Res Pub Health (16) 2022
Chen H and Seng Z. When do Hedonic and Eudaimonic Orientations Lead to Happiness? Moderating Effects of Orientation Priority. Int J Res Public Health, September 2021
[81] Domencio SI and Ryan RM. The Emerging Neuroscience of Intrinsic Motivation: A New Frontier in Self-Determination Research. Front Hum Neuroci, March 2015
[82] Gabriel M. Why the World Does Not Exists. Polity Publishers, 2017
THE PARADOX OF SELF-CONSCIOUSNESS. A conversation with Marcus Gabriel in "Conversation" edge.org website July 2023

and purposes influence the daily values, choices, and decisions.

To develop optimal health sustainably, it is essential to rely on values and attitudes that promote life-affirming orientations and lifestyle choices that enhance health. To align human life with deeper fulfillment, there must be an acknowledgment of the inherent abilities of one's spiritual nature. Evidence from life shows that today's materialism, consumerism, and hedonism weaken the spiritual dimension of life. The material path in human life adversely affects people's consciousness and health. It masks the importance of spiritual health and self-evolution.

When caught in the trap of the acquisitive mindset—without knowing when enough is enough—people make poor choices, set wrong priorities, and lead unhealthy lifestyles. This situation is worsened by the advertising industry, which effectively distorts people's understanding of their true human nature. It undercuts the spiritual dimension of human existence. Materialism and consumerism damage the spiritual side of human life. The acquisitive mindset today is the biggest barrier to living a balanced, whole life. We have developed a way of life where we chase one pleasure after another. Ordinary people find it almost impossible to stay focused on what truly matters in life.

If we are not indifferent, we may be unaware that we live disoriented, unsettled, and without a clear spiritual or moral foundation in our lives. This has led to the emergence of a "new" human reality, characterized by a lack of solid, strong, and stable personhood. We have distorted what it means to be human and what it is to truly be human. For example, utilitarian individualism is deeply embedded in our way of being human. It is increasingly becoming a dominant human tendency. This is visible in the everyday behaviors of the "you-use-me-and-I-use-you" culture of today. As a result, it has become second nature to conceal past wrongdoings and shortcomings by twisting the truth, telling half-truths, or misrepresenting reality. We vigilantly guard and cleverly protect this pseudo-self, using cover-ups to survive. We tend to approach our fellow humans as if they are aliens because we have become unsure of who people really are.

Today, what we are fundamentally experiencing and witnessing is a "new" human reality. It is marked by a deep emptiness inside. The void people feel daily is reflected in countless moments through speech, behavior, relationship patterns, life pursuits, and more. Material prosperity and wealth accumulation, for their own sake, seem like a helpless attempt to fill that inner void. In many subtle ways, the void reveals a spiritual sickness. Our chaotic, tumultuous world exposes the wounded human spirit of our humanity.

We live in a world where people are confused about what truly matters or how to live. We ignore how we complicate life for ourselves and others. We fail to recognize the connection between our lifestyles and the harmful effects they have on everyday human life around the world. We don't wrestle with what it means to be human. This has made us indifferent to harming ourselves, others, humanity, and the planet. The "new" human reality is turning the world upside down.

We are tragically depriving ourselves of the holistic human life that we can have. It won't happen unless we regularly tune into the inner workings of our minds to confront our core reality and stay true to our authentic selves. It will happen when we develop the natural spiritual abilities of human nature. It depends on how committed we are each day to nurturing spiritual health. It results from intentional efforts toward self-evolution, not from the magic of celestial powers.

In the face of all the devastating effects of humanity's material-focused path dominating our lives, we sadly neglect engaging with our spiritual potential. We have become accustomed to living without acknowledging the spiritual aspect of human nature, thereby dismissing the importance of spiritual health. Essentially, what we are doing today is ignoring our innate abilities like intuition, wisdom, and perception. We are badly misguided in how we live, unaware of how this will ultimately impact us. Every day, little by little, we move closer to the edge of catastrophic destruction.

We appear indifferent to the disastrous and destructive problems, collectively caused, that threaten the future of humanity and the planet. It's all talk and no action to stop the increasingly frequent environmental crises caused by the disruption we've inflicted on the natural order. Truth be told, we don't care about spiritual well-being, a better quality of human life, a healthier humanity, or a healthier planet.

Experts in human consciousness believe that the normal tension between material and spiritual standards of human life is effectively managed when one remains true to the real self.[83] The inner-core reality and the real self are always deeply and intricately involved in the meaning and purpose of life, influencing one's life orientation and goals. However, in our times, people are experiencing a more diffuse, amorphous, and deregulated sense of meaning and purpose in life.

Every day, ordinary people's minds face mental confusion and chaotic thinking patterns. Cultural pressures, influences, and standards often do not align with the pursuit of higher ideals, purposes, the common good, and spiritual growth. The instinctual and emotional processes of consciousness usually block the brain's mechanisms for learning from experiences.

Self-views, life-views, and worldviews are shaped by the dominant cultural script that favors the pseudo-self. The spirit of individualism, consumerism, and hedonism weakens the true self. Global cultural phenomena compete with people's innate human instincts, insights, and intuitions. The modern cultural environment hinders the development of our inherent "spiritual capacities." A person's human consciousness is often limited by brain systems that prioritize the instinctual-emotional sensitivities of the sensual, hedonic, and fleeting aspects of life. The deeper insights and clearer perspectives of the "intuitive mind" are suppressed by the "sensual mind,"

Today, we operate with cultural antennas and blinders that make us

---

[83] Kaebnick GE. Humans in Nature: The World as We Find it and the World as We create it. Oxford University Press, 2011

unaware of the current depraved spiritual and moral condition of humanity. Numerous illusions and delusions of success and happiness obscure the genuine experiences of life and reality. We cling to childish fantasies about human existence. There is an unwavering indifference to the long-term effects of our lifestyle on both humanity and the planet. This prompts the question: Have the human brain's systems for higher consciousness been disrupted?

To sum up:

In our world, success driven by possession is very persuasive. It has effectively blinded us to what truly matters in life. It fosters the "I-me-mine" mindset, which normalizes the idea that some people are entitled to excess while others lack basic necessities. It narrows our life perspectives and hampers common sense about the common good.

The culture of extravagance and accumulation is promoted by the capitalist economic system and the advertising industry that dominates it. There is no way to escape the ads in our world that constantly convince us we are not enough and lack something. Ads relentlessly bombard us with subliminal messages, making us believe there's more to acquire and achieve for success and happiness. Ads define the "good life" in terms of wealth, stardom, and raw power.

Furthermore, in our society, the culture of stardom and glamour has led us to associate the "good life" with popularity and fame. Social idols become the ultimate standard for happiness and success. For everyday people, pop culture stars and celebrities are seen as the top models of achievement and joy. This focus causes people to concentrate on superficial and shallow appearances, only to feel more dwarfed and dehumanized by it.

The culture of fame and glamour floods us with subliminal messages that we need the pseudo-self. It has turned human life into an enterprise of what is fake and unpredictable. People's social appearances overshadow the importance of their true selves. They struggle to accept and embrace their true selves, often denying that one exists. We have mastered the art of hiding our failings and wrongdoings. We build the "good life" on a foundation of secrets and self-deceptions. Today, it is difficult to truly know or sense who a person really is.

In daily life, people often mistake the pseudo-self for the true self. Although the pseudo-self remains in survival mode, they live their lives under its influence. They carefully protect the pseudo-self by maintaining social appearances, which daily foster habits focused on face-saving rather than truth-seeking; ego investment rather than personal growth; achieving rather than cooperation; acquiring rather than sharing; and self-centeredness rather than consideration for others.

A person's self-understanding and self-acceptance are based on what they imagine as their true self. The genuine human worth of a person gets overshadowed by what is trivial, hollow, and superficial. The better version of oneself—a holistic human being—is not part of the "good life." We give up the natural healing processes—the "renewal energy"—that rely on the freedom of the human spirit animated by the real self.

The acquisitive mindset and pseudo-self weaken the "freedoms" we desire every day. Possession-focused success, the pursuit of pleasure, and the pseudo-self constantly limit the "freedoms" that everyone most seeks in life today. Life experiences teach us that nowadays, everyone yearns for freedom from stress and despair, freedom from anxiety and guilt, freedom from physical and mental health issues, freedom from hypocrisy and double standards, freedom from malicious and corrupt actions, freedom from obsessive desire for more, and the madness of endless enslavement, and the list goes on.

The human spirit withers without the "freedoms' we all desperately desire. Spiritual wounds are the unavoidable result of lacking these freedoms. The battered and wounded human spirit is a constant presence in daily life.

The "freedoms" we long for can only come when the innate spiritual nature of humans is recognized as part of human life, guiding us through existence, and when spiritual health is included in what makes a "good life."

Then, the material side of human nature is understood for what it does to us—hindering true inner freedom. To grow truly free from within, we must pay attention to what really matters during the brief life we have. We need to confront the metaphysical realities of human life.

The withering, wretched, broken, and wounded human spirit of our times constantly calls us to find freedom from within. This call is about realizing that through voluntary simplicity, high-mindedness, and virtuous living, we can experience freedom from the inside, leading to deeper, healthier living and a more fulfilling human life. The invitation is to focus on our innate spiritual nature and to recognize the spiritual dimension of life in order to live with clear perspectives, values, and goals. It is also a call to include spiritual well-being as part of the pursuit of the "good life"—the kind of life fulfillment every person deserves, not the empty one we often chase and attain today.

When people develop spiritual health, they focus on the true self and are better supported in finding correct life perspectives. They realize that the "good life" is like balancing on a tightrope. They grow in their intention to practice simple living for the greater good. They emphasize correct thinking and higher ideals, cultivate relationships with life-affirming goals, and improve daily health care management. They find standards other than material ones to measure themselves and others.

Simple living recognizes that the only way to engage in life truly is by understanding our metaphysical human nature—the innate spiritual aspect and awareness of the spiritual dimension of life. People realize that this metaphysical human nature helps them stay focused on what truly matters, making it an art to build, maintain, and restore spiritual health each day. They promote a lifestyle that values healthy habits, minimizes wants, and works for the common good. When they resist hunger pangs or reject selfish ambitions, they nurture their spiritual health through everyday practices of simplicity. Living simply always fosters spiritual growth every day we live.

The tension between our material and spiritual human natures will inevitably be experienced in daily life. This fact has been recognized since ancient times. Iconic historical figures such as Mahavir, Buddha, Confucius, Lao Tze, Jesus, Muhammad, and many others—who served as models of noble spiritual human nature to their contemporaries and to countless generations afterward—highlighted the truth in their teachings.

Spiritual health develops through the dynamic relationship between the true self and real-life experiences. When the true self is active in creating and fulfilling human life, one tends to invest less in pretending, cover-ups, and face-saving than when life centers on the pseudo-self. Likewise, one is less focused on managing, planning, sorting, and controlling when life is driven by greed, possession, and the accumulation of wealth—things that only create illusions of the "good life."

The pseudo-self in daily life is at the heart of many serious issues that threaten the health of individuals, society, humanity, and the planet. The cumulative effect of people's unhealthy spiritual core and pseudo-self gradually harms human well-being and poses significant risks to the planet.

In conclusion, when we embrace simple living, we eliminate everything but what is truly essential and focus on what genuinely matters. We discard distractions that divert us from the soul-numbing pursuit of human life. The fat cat's self-indulgence in wealth and extravagance is seen as an external sign of human decadence. We find the meaning and purpose of life not through external prosperity, but through "spiritual prosperity" of wholeness and a wholesome way of life. This kind of prosperity is deeply internal and can never be lost. It is always experienced as a more profound sense of joy, freedom, fulfillment, and contentment. It manifests through love, compassion, altruism, high-mindedness, humaneness, and all that reflects the human essence in daily life. The noble human nature always keeps focus on what is more important and relevant to the well-being of humanity and the planet. The goal is the common good and cultivating a more vibrant life. We do not waste time and energy on the frivolous, trivial, or fleeting. All of this describes how spiritual health feels in the everyday life of an ordinary person.

CONCLUSION

In a world fraught with numerous dangers for humanity, the scientific community and 'enlightened' citizens are shining a spotlight on spiritual health. It is recognized as a vital and fundamental part of human life, the future of humanity, and the planet. No other time in history has seen more focus on the human spiritual phenomenon than in the past few decades. Voices are growing louder in the global community, and scientific research is increasing to highlight the urgency and importance of spiritual health in human life.

Today, the historical connection between religion and the spiritual has been broken, and most people no longer associate religion with spiritual health. The spiritual is seen as innate within humans, and every person is inseparable from the spiritual, whether or not they follow a religion. It is also recognized that the spiritual aspect of health, like the physical, is a practical concept that must be nurtured daily for optimal health.

Today, we have a deeper understanding of how the human spirit supports optimal health and positively influences society's well-being. Many research studies show a strong link between spiritual health and overall personal health. When people focus on their spiritual health, they develop a clearer understanding of their relationships with others and a greater sense of interconnectedness with the universe. The benefits of spiritual health have been scientifically confirmed, and it's evident that it plays a vital role in creating a healthier planet and humanity.

Over the past century, technological advances in medicine have led to significant changes in healthcare but have also shifted the focus from a care-oriented approach to a treatment-based, technology-driven model. However, in recent decades, the healthcare industry, the scientific community, scholars, and professionals have begun to reestablish balance in healthcare by reconnecting with medicine's deeper roots for healing—namely, the human spirit.

There is a growing sense of urgency among scientists, scholars, social reformers, and healthcare professionals to help people find a peaceful and balanced place within themselves for daily harmony. They believe that spiritual health influences a wide range of outcomes for individuals, society, humanity, the environment, and the planet.

Like other aspects of health, spiritual health varies over a lifetime, with peaks that highlight the soul's landscape and valleys that require effort to climb out of, especially during times of excessive self-centeredness and self-indulgence. Neglecting to nurture spiritual health diminishes the ability to practice self-restraint, maintain inner balance and equanimity, and foster love, empathy, and forgiveness. Generally, it becomes more difficult to find peace and happiness in life. These elements are connected to all aspects of health through thoughts, emotions, and actions. Numerous research studies show that physical and mental health often decline when individuals do not actively nurture their spiritual health.

For many people, spiritual health becomes important during times of illness and aging. There is a situational urgency that shifts their focus to vital aspects of spiritual health – the inner-core reality, the true self, and life's meaning and purpose – for endurance, comfort, and strength. This stage of life presents challenges related to declining physical and mental abilities and leads to perceptions that were previously unnoticed. They begin to recognize deeper connections they had missed earlier in life. However, in the years gone by, there have been missed opportunities to benefit from spiritual health. Few realize the unfortunate timing for friends and family to start their journey toward spiritual well-being.

Spiritual health mainly stems from the deepest aspirations of life, the human quest for purpose and meaning. A person's purpose and meaning are shaped, influenced, and controlled by their inner core. This inner core is a strong central connection within the individual that can initiate and develop the aspect of spiritual health, as well as other health components. It also serves as the link between the person and others, and the world around them. The inner core can also trigger and create conditions of "spiritual disease" that harm a person and affect others.

The frequent reports of sociopathic behaviors and psychopathic crimes in the media highlight an ongoing decline in the inner core, the true self, and people's spiritual health. This decline is more often observed in the home, workplace, places of worship, the marketplace, and nearly everywhere else. There are often desperate cries in our times, urging the world to restore the soul in life. It is the call to recover the inner core and connect with the authentic self to reach the higher self. This indicates that cultivating spiritual health is just as crucial for high-functioning members of society as it is for the so-called "identified patients" in our communities.

www.ingramcontent.com/pod-product-compliance
Lightning Source LLC
LaVergne TN
LVHW010218070526
838199LV00062B/4650